Rail-Trails
Washington
& Oregon

🦫 **WILDERNESS PRESS** . . . *on the trail since 1967*

Rail-Trails: Washington and Oregon
1st Edition
Copyright © 2015 by Rails-to-Trails Conservancy

Maps: Lohnes+Wright; Map data: Environmental Systems Research Institute
Cover design: Scott McGrew
Book design: Annie Long

Library of Congress Cataloging-in-Publication Data

Rail-trails Washington and Oregon : the official rails-to-trails conservancy guidebook / by
The Rails-to-Trails Conservancy. — 1st edition.
    pages cm
 Includes bibliographical references and index.
 ISBN 978-0-89997-793-5 (alk. paper) — ISBN 0-89997-793-6 (alk. paper)
 1. Rail-trails—Washington (State)—Guidebooks. 2. Rail-trails—Oregon—Guidebooks.
3. Outdoor recreation—Washington (State)—Guidebooks. 4. Outdoor recreation—
Oregon—Guidebooks. 5. Washington (State)—Guidebooks. 6. Oregon—Guidebooks.
I. Rails-to-Trails Conservancy, issuing body.
 GV191.42.W2R35 2015
 796.509797—dc23

                    2015009027

ISBN: 978-0-89997-793-5; eISBN: 978-0-89997-794-2

Manufactured in the United States of America

Published by: **Wilderness Press**
                 Keen Communications
                 PO Box 43673
                 Birmingham, AL 35243
                 800-443-7227; fax 205-326-1012
                 info@wildernesspress.com
                 wildernesspress.com

Visit our website for a complete listing of our books and for ordering information.

Distributed by Publishers Group West

Front cover: Astoria Riverwalk, © Karl Wirsing
Back cover: Similkameen Trail, © Ted Murray

SAFETY NOTICE: Although Wilderness Press and Rails-to-Trails Conservancy have
made every attempt to ensure that the information in this book is accurate at press time,
they are not responsible for any loss, damage, injury, or inconvenience that may occur to
anyone while using this book. You are responsible for your own safety and health while in
the wilderness. The fact that a trail is described in this book does not mean that it will be
safe for you. Be aware that trail conditions can change from day to day. Always check local
conditions, know your own limitations, and consult a map.

About Rails-to-Trails Conservancy

Headquartered in Washington, D.C., Rails-to-Trails Conservancy (RTC) is a nonprofit organization dedicated to creating a nationwide network of trails from former rail lines and connecting corridors to build healthier places for healthier people.

Railways helped build America. Spanning from coast to coast, these ribbons of steel linked people, communities, and enterprises, spurring commerce and forging a single nation that bridges a continent. But in recent decades, many of these routes have fallen into disuse, severing communal ties that helped bind Americans together.

When RTC opened its doors in 1986, the rail-trail movement was in its infancy. While there were some 250 miles of open rail-trails in the United States, most projects focused on single, linear routes in rural areas, created for recreation and conservation. RTC sought broader protection for the unused corridors, incorporating rural, suburban, and urban routes.

Year after year, RTC's efforts to protect and align public funding with trail building created an environment that allowed trail advocates in communities across the country to initiate trail projects. These ever-growing ranks of trail professionals, volunteers, and RTC supporters have built momentum for the national rail-trails movement. As the number of supporters multiplied, so did the rail-trails.

Americans now enjoy more than 22,000 miles of open rail-trails, and as they flock to the trails to connect with family members and friends, enjoy nature, and get to places in their local neighborhoods and beyond, their economic prosperity, health, and overall well-being continue to flourish.

A signature endeavor of RTC is **TrailLink.com,** America's portal to these rail-trails as well as other multiuse trails. When RTC launched **TrailLink.com** in 2000, our organization was one of the first to compile such detailed trail information on a national scale. Today, the website continues to play a critical role in both encouraging and satisfying the country's growing need for opportunities to ride, walk, skate, or run for recreation or transportation. This free trail-finder database—which includes detailed descriptions, interactive maps, photo galleries, and first-hand ratings and reviews—can be used as a companion resource to the trails in this guidebook.

The national voice for more than 160,000 members and supporters, RTC is committed to ensuring a better future for America, made possible by trails and the connections they inspire. Learn more at **railstotrails.org.**

CANADA

BRITISH COLUMBIA

○ VANCOUVER

○ SEATTLE
WASHINGTON
see page 6

○ Olympia

PORTLAND ○

○ Salem

OREGON
see page 118

N

0   50   100 miles

rails·to·trails
conservancy

Table of Contents

WASHINGTON 6

OREGON 118

Staff Picks

Staff members at Rails-to-Trails Conservancy handpicked the following trails as their favorites, based on such merits as scenic value, unique attractions, bike-friendly communities, and excellent maintenance of the trails and their trailside amenities.

Washington

Oregon

Foreword

For those of you who have already experienced the sheer enjoyment and freedom of riding on a rail-trail, welcome back! You'll find *Rail-Trails: Washington and Oregon* to be a useful and fun guide to your favorite trails, as well as an introduction to pathways you have yet to travel.

For readers who are discovering for the first time the adventures possible on a rail-trail, thank you for joining the rail-trail movement. Since 1986, Rails-to-Trails Conservancy has been the leading supporter and defender of these priceless public corridors. We are excited to bring you *Rail-Trails: Washington and Oregon,* so you, too, can enjoy this region's rail-trails. These hiking and biking trails are ideal ways to connect with your community, with nature, and with your friends and family.

I've found that trails have a way of bringing people together; as you'll see from this book, you have opportunities in every state you visit to get on a great trail. Whether you're looking for a place to exercise, explore, commute, or play, there is a trail in this book for you.

So I invite you to sit back, relax, pick a trail that piques your interest—and then get out, get active, and have some fun. I'll be out on the trails too, so be sure to wave as you go by.

Happy trails,
Keith Laughlin, President
Rails-to-Trails Conservancy

Acknowledgments

Many thanks to the following contributors and to all the trail managers we called on for assistance to ensure the maps, photographs, and trail descriptions are as accurate as possible:

Mia Barbara

Gene Bisbee

Cindy Dickerson

Eli Griffen

Kathryn Harris

Amber Kaye Henderson

Amy Kapp

Barbara Richey

Timothy Rosner

Laura Stark

Beautiful views await on the Wallace Falls Railway Trail in Washington (see page 105).

Introduction

Of the more than 1,900 rail-trails across the United States, 42 are highlighted in *Rail-Trails: Washington and Oregon*. These paths tread storied routes of westward expansion and industrialization, spurred by timber and coal, and offer a glimpse into life a century ago. They still bear the signatures of their history: tunnels, trestles, raised berms, and depots, communities born and abandoned.

Some of the original railroads in the Northwest served as logging lines through the massive forests of Oregon and Washington. Rail-trails retrace their tracks, as well as those of other passenger and freight lines. Their original purposes and destinations vary, but each of these rail-trails joins past with present, creating a living memorial of the corridors that helped shape the region.

Washington State boasts some of the most rural and unique rail-trails in the country. These are not always the flat and even pathways you might expect from rail-trails; for example, the John Wayne Pioneer Trail (Milwaukee Road Corridor) offers a backcountry adventure as it traverses the state. Complementing these rustic pathways are paved trails, such as the Chehalis Western Trail or the well-groomed Foothills Trail, which features views of Mount Rainier during much of its length.

In a region best known for rain and gray skies, the Olympic Discovery Trail bucks the trend. The trail passes through Sequim, a town shrouded in the infamous rain shadow of the northern Olympic Peninsula. The town claims far less rain than other coastal towns, which makes travel by bike or foot along the route even more enjoyable.

Oregon's trails are as diverse as the state itself. Its arid central region is showcased along the 17-mile Deschutes River Railbed Trail, while the Astoria Riverwalk is the place to go for those who want to experience the maritime history that the state is equally known for. In addition, the trails in this guidebook range from rural to urban, and many options in between. It may be hard to believe that bike paths in Portland are in the same state as the Lewis and Clark Commemorative Trail, a 7-mile adventure that traverses cliffs above the Columbia River. While only 9 of the 42 trails in this guidebook are in the Beaver State, each one is sure to inspire you and leave you longing to return.

This guidebook includes not one but two trails that have been inducted into the Rail-Trail Hall of Fame. Seattle is home to the Burke-Gilman Trail, a 17-mile corridor that was inducted in 2008. Oregon's Springwater Corridor earned the distinction in 2011 and is an integral part of Portland's bike and pedestrian trail network.

No matter which route in *Rail-Trails: Washington and Oregon* you decide to try, you'll be touching on the heart of the community that helped build it and the history that first brought the rails to the region.

What Is a Rail-Trail?

Rail-trails are multiuse public paths built along former railroad corridors. Most often flat or following a gentle grade, they are suited to walking, running, cycling, mountain biking, in-line skating, cross-country skiing, horseback riding, and wheelchair use. Since the 1960s, Americans have created more than 22,000 miles of rail-trails throughout the country.

These extremely popular recreation and transportation corridors traverse urban, suburban, and rural landscapes. Many preserve historic landmarks, while others serve as wildlife conservation corridors, linking isolated parks and establishing greenways in developed areas. Rail-trails also stimulate local economies by boosting tourism and promoting trailside businesses.

What Is a Rail-with-Trail?

A rail-with-trail is a public path that parallels a still-active rail line. Some run adjacent to high-speed, scheduled trains, often linking public transportation stations, while others follow tourist routes and slow-moving excursion trains. Many share an easement, separated from the rails by extensive fencing. More than 240 rails-with-trails currently exist in the United States.

How to Use This Book

*R*ail-Trails: Washington and Oregon provides the information you'll need to plan a rewarding rail-trail trek. With words to inspire you and maps to chart your path, it makes choosing the best route a breeze. Following are some of the highlights.

Maps

You'll find three levels of maps in this book: an **overall regional map, state locator maps,** and **detailed trail maps.**

Each chapter details a particular state's network of trails, marked on locator maps in the chapter introduction. Use these maps to find the trails nearest you, or select several neighboring trails and plan a weekend hiking or biking excursion. Once you find a trail on a state locator map, simply flip to the corresponding page number for a full description. Accompanying trail maps mark each route's access roads, trailheads, parking areas, restrooms, and other defining features.

Key to Map Icons

Parking

Drinking water

Restrooms

Trail Descriptions

Trails are listed in alphabetical order within each chapter. Each description leads off with a set of summary information, including trail endpoints and mileage, a roughness index, the trail surface, and possible uses.

The map and summary information list the trail endpoints (either a city, street, or more specific location), with suggested points from which to start and finish. Additional access points are marked on the maps and mentioned in the trail descriptions. The maps and descriptions also highlight available amenities, including parking and restrooms, as well as such area attractions as shops, services, museums, parks, and stadiums. Trail length is listed in miles.

Each trail bears a roughness index rating from 1 to 3. A rating of 1 indicates a smooth, level surface that is accessible to users of all ages and abilities. A 2 rating means the surface may be loose and/or uneven and could pose a problem for road bikes and wheelchairs. A 3 rating suggests a rough surface that is only recommended for mountain bikers and hikers. Surfaces can range from asphalt or concrete to ballast, cinder, crushed stone, gravel, grass, dirt, and/or sand. Where relevant, trail descriptions address alternating surface conditions.

All trails are open to pedestrians, and most allow bicycles, except where noted in the trail summary or description. The summary also indicates wheelchair access. Other possible uses include in-line skating, fishing, horseback riding, mountain biking, and cross-country skiing. While most trails are off-limits to motor vehicles, some local trail organizations do allow all-terrain vehicles and snowmobiles.

Trail descriptions themselves suggest an ideal itinerary for each route, including the best parking areas and access points, where to begin, your direction of travel, and any highlights along the way. The text notes any connecting or neighboring routes, with page numbers for the respective trail descriptions. Following each description are directions to the recommended trailheads.

Each trail description also lists a local website for further information. Be sure to visit these websites in advance for updates and current conditions. **TrailLink.com** is another great resource for updated content on the trails in this guidebook.

Trail Use

Rail-trails are popular destinations for a range of users, often making them busy places to enjoy the outdoors. Following basic trail etiquette and safety guidelines will make your experience more pleasant.

- ➤ **Keep to the right,** except when passing.
- ➤ **Pass on the left,** and give a clear audible warning: "Passing on your left."
- ➤ **Be aware** of other trail users, particularly around corners and blind spots, and be especially careful when entering a trail, changing direction, or passing, so that you don't collide with traffic.
- ➤ **Respect** wildlife and public and private property; leave no trace and take out litter.
- ➤ **Control your speed,** especially near pedestrians, playgrounds, and heavily congested areas.
- ➤ **Travel single file.** Cyclists and pedestrians should ride or walk single file in congested areas or areas with reduced visibility.
- ➤ **Cross carefully** at intersections; always look both ways and yield to through traffic. Pedestrians have the right-of-way.
- ➤ **Keep one ear open and volume low** on portable listening devices to increase your awareness of your surroundings.
- ➤ **Wear a helmet** and other safety gear if you're cycling or in-line skating.

➤ **Consider visibility.** Wear reflective clothing, use bicycle lights, or bring flashlights or helmet-mounted lights for tunnel passages or twilight excursions.

➤ **Keep moving,** and don't block the trail. When taking a rest, turn off the trail to the right. Groups should avoid congregating on or blocking the trails. If you have an accident on the trail, move to the right as soon as possible.

➤ **Bicyclists yield** to all other trail users. Pedestrians yield to horses. If in doubt, yield to all other trail users.

➤ **Dogs are permitted** on most trails, **but some trails through parks, wildlife refuges, or other sensitive areas may not allow pets; it's best to check the trail website before your visit. If pets are permitted, keep your dog** on a short leash and under your control at all times. Remove dog waste in a designated trash receptacle.

➤ **Teach your children** these trail essentials, and be especially diligent to keep them out of faster-moving trail traffic.

➤ **Be prepared,** especially on long-distance rural trails. Bring water, snacks, maps, a light source, matches, and other equipment you may need. Because some areas may not have good reception for mobile phones, know where you're going, and tell someone else your plan.

Key to Trail Use

| cycling | in-line skating | fishing | wheel-chair access | horse-back riding | mountain biking | walking | cross-country skiing |

Learn More

While *Rail-Trails: Washington and Oregon* is a helpful guide to available routes in the region, it wasn't feasible to list every rail-trail in these two states, and new trails spring up each year. To learn about additional rail-trails in your area or to plan a trip to an area beyond the scope of this book, visit Rails-to-Trails Conservancy's trail-finder website, **TrailLink.com**—a free resource with information on more than 30,000 miles of trails nationwide.

Washington

1. Bill Chipman Palouse Trail
2. Burke-Gilman Trail
3. Cascade Trail
4. Cedar River Trail
5. Centennial Trail State Park
6. Chehalis Western Trail
7. Coal Creek Trail
8. Cowiche Canyon Trail
9. East Lake Sammamish Trail
10. Elliott Bay Trail (Terminal 91 Bike Path)
11. Fish Lake Trail
12. Foothills Trail
13. Interurban Trail (Bellingham)
14. Interurban Trail (North)
15. Interurban Trail (South)
16. Issaquah-Preston Trail
17. John Wayne Pioneer Trail (Milwaukee Road Corridor)
18. Klickitat Trail
19. Lower Yakima Valley Pathway
20. Olympic Discovery Trail: Blyn to Elwha River
21. Olympic Discovery Trail: Port Townsend
22. Olympic Discovery Trail: Spruce Railroad Trail
23. Preston-Snoqualmie Trail
24. Sammamish River Trail
25. Similkameen Trail
26. Snohomish County Centennial Trail
27. Snoqualmie Valley Trail
28. South Bay Trail
29. Tommy Thompson Trail
30. Wallace Falls Railway Trail
31. Willapa Hills Trail
32. Woodland Trail
33. Yelm-Tenino Trail

rails-to-trails
conservancy

Washington

The Wallace Falls Railway Trail (see page 105) welcomes you to the lush Pacific Northwest.

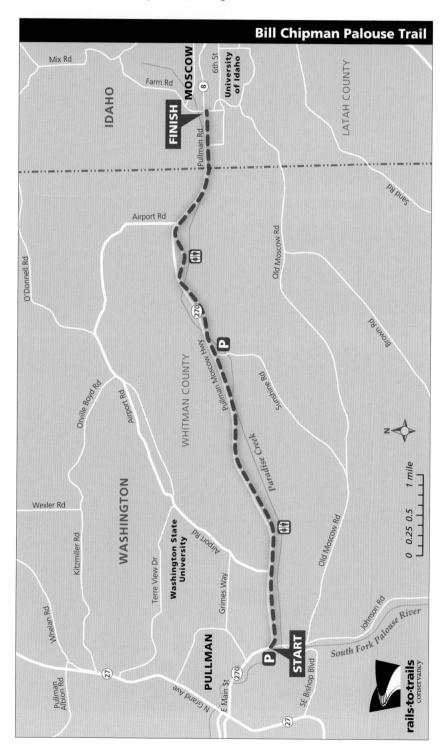

The Bill Chipman Palouse Trail stretches 7.1 miles through the rolling wheat fields of the Palouse region, offering a convenient, paved connection between Washington State University and the University of Idaho.

The trail follows a piece of corridor from the former Union Pacific Railroad (constructed by the Columbia & Palouse Railroad in 1885), which transported passengers from Colfax to Moscow. The last passenger train ran in 1957. Now, the wide, mostly flat pathway—a respite from the area's many hills and valleys—accommodates non-motorized users of all types, with additional trail connections at either end.

Along the route from Pullman to Moscow, 13 original railroad bridges cross Paradise Creek. Opportunities abound to spot birds and other forms of aquatic wildlife

Counties
Latah (ID), Whitman

Endpoints
SE Bishop Blvd.
(Pullman, WA) to
Farm Road (Moscow, ID)

Mileage
7.1

Roughness Index
1

Surface
Asphalt

Crossing state lines and directly linking two universities, this trail bridges the 7-mile gap between Pullman, Washington, and Moscow, Idaho.

thriving in and near the water. Trail users will also find emergency phones, restrooms accessible for people with disabilities, benches, bike racks, and interpretive signs describing the history, agriculture, and ecology of the region.

The Bill Chipman Palouse Trail overlaps with the Pullman Loop Trail for approximately 1 mile, starting near the Chipman trailhead at Bishop Boulevard. From here, you'll cross Paradise Creek to a cirque of benches and an interpretive station at Birdhouse Depot. Magpies are common; the stream also provides a habitat for hawks, falcons, and more than 100 other bird species.

As you travel farther along the gentle uphill grade, you'll come to the next point of interest, a giant grain elevator. A greenway buffers you from the four-lane highway to Moscow, as do the lovely waysides with interpretive signs and benches along the corridor. Grab some water at Neil Wayside near Pullman. This dry, unsheltered path is often windy heading eastward.

The trail culminates at Farm Road in Moscow. Continue east on the 2-mile Paradise Path through the north and east edges of the University of Idaho campus and up Paradise Creek to the Moscow city limits. Here, you can connect with the paved, 12-mile Latah Trail to Troy, Idaho.

CONTACT: tinyurl.com/billchipman

DIRECTIONS

To get to the west end of the trail from US 195 near Pullman, WA, take WA 270 for 3.4 miles (following signs to remain on WA 270), and turn south (right) onto Bishop Blvd. (From the east, Bishop Blvd. is at the first light going into town.) After approximately two blocks, turn left into a small parking area. The trail begins at Bishop Blvd. Parking in Pullman is available at the Quality Inn lot or on Derby St. near Koppel Farm.

To get to the Moscow, ID, trailhead from US 195 near Pullman, WA, take WA 270 (ID 8) approximately 11 miles into Moscow. Turn north (left) at Farm Road, and park in the Palouse Mall parking lot. Cross back over ID 8, and go west onto the path. All property to the south of ID 8 is part of the University of Idaho and not available for public parking.

2 Burke-Gilman Trail

The Burke-Gilman Trail is as much a thoroughfare for commuting to work and the University of Washington as it is a staple for social recreation and fitness. Built in the 1970s, the trail was among the first rail-trails in the country and helped inspire dozens of similar projects around the nation.

Golden Gardens Park and the Sammamish River Trail mark the boundaries of the Burke-Gilman Trail, once a line of the Seattle, Lake Shore and Eastern Railway (SLS&E). Created in 1885 by two prominent Seattle residents, Thomas Burke and Daniel Gilman, the SLS&E was purchased by the Northern Pacific Railroad in 1901. Heavy traffic by the logging industry sustained the line through 1963, and the corridor became inactive in 1971. The heavy traffic continues as trail users make their way from Puget Sound to Lake Union and Lake Washington.

County
King

Endpoints
Golden Gardens Park at Seaview Ave. NW (Seattle) to 102nd Ave. NE near Woodinville Dr./ WA 522 (Bothell)

Mileage
18.8

Roughness Index
1

Surface
Asphalt

Inducted into Rails-to-Trails Conservancy's Rail-Trail Hall of Fame, the Burke-Gilman Trail is a must-visit during any trip to Seattle.

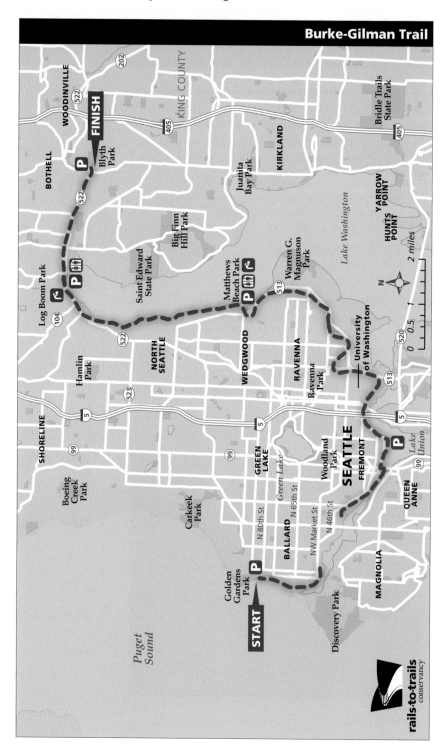

Burke-Gilman Trail

You can start your journey at Puget Sound at the Golden Gardens Park entrance, on the east side of Seaview Avenue Northwest. Reach the Northwest 60th Street Viewpoint by traversing the waterfront and marina for just over a mile. Signs direct you to cross Seaview Avenue and head 0.7 mile to the Ballard Locks. The sidewalk along Seaview Avenue, now Northwest 54th Street, connects to Northwest Market Street in downtown Ballard. To reach the 1-mile on-road portion of the missing trail link, turn right at Shilshole Avenue Northwest. Turn left onto Northwest Vernon Place, and then turn right onto Ballard Avenue Northwest. A right onto 17th Avenue Northwest returns you to Shilshole Avenue, where the road is painted for cyclists and becomes Northwest 45th Street after crossing under the Ballard Bridge. Return to the sidewalk and trail at 11th Avenue Northwest and 45th. Leaving Puget Sound, you will find yourself in a park beside the Fremont Canal that connects the sound to Lake Union. Past the steps waits Fremont, a great area for food, gelato, a glimpse of the famous Fremont Rocket, a Vladimir Lenin statue, and an infamous troll statue. This brings you to Lake Union, 5 miles from Golden Gardens Park. The trail turns right onto North Northlake Way at North 34th Street, guiding you to the historic waterfront of a former coal gasification plant, Gas Works Park, where kite flying and kayaking are popular. Next stop: University of Washington, but not before the orange *Wall of Death* (an art installation representing a motorcycle velodrome).

Circling around the U District (so named for the University of Washington) and retail area at mile 7 will put you on a secluded path of maples, dogwoods, and occasional firs. You'll then pass above the waterfront Magnuson Park at Northeast 70th Street, a former naval station next to the National Oceanic Atmospheric Administration. At mile 13, a bridge crosses Sand Point Way Northeast. To your right lies Seattle's largest freshwater swimming beach, Matthews Beach Park.

Lakeside homes on tiny streets line the trail beyond. The city of Lake Forest Park welcomes you at mile 16, where you'll pass a serpent fountain and a mural as you parallel Bothell Way Northeast/WA 522. Two lakefront parks provide a respite from this 3-mile commercial district. At Ballinger Way Northeast/WA 104, look toward the lake for the tiny Lyon Creek Waterfront Preserve. Tracy Owen Station, also known as Log Boom Park, is the last lakefront stop, offering restrooms, a water fountain, a play area, and history.

Leave the roadside at the north end of Lake Washington for the riverfront. At mile 20, you can head straight over a bridge into Blyth Park or fork left to continue onto the Sammamish River Trail. Buses will return you to Ballard, or you can continue to the east side of Lake Washington and onto Snoqualmie Valley or to the Columbia River.

CONTACT: seattle.gov/transportation/BGT.htm

DIRECTIONS

To reach Golden Gardens Park from I-5, take Exit 172 to N. 85th St., and head west 3.4 miles to 32nd Ave. NW. Turn right onto 32nd Ave. NW, and continue on Golden Gardens Dr. NW for 0.8 mile. Turn left onto Seaview Pl. NW, which meets Seaview Ave. NW and a parking lot in 0.2 mile. Disability parking is available.

To reach Blyth Park from I-405, take Exit 23 to WA 522 west toward Seattle. After 0.2 mile, bear right onto Kaysner Way. Turn left onto Main St. After 0.1 mile, turn left onto 102nd Ave. NE. When the road ends at 0.3 mile, turn right onto W. Riverside Dr. Blyth Park is 0.5 mile ahead.

The 22.5-mile Cascade Trail—boasting 12 benches, 23 trestles, and two bridges made from repurposed railcars—follows the Skagit River as it parallels WA 20 into the Cascade foothills of northwest Washington (ending in Concrete). The trail, completed in 1999, claims its origins from the Great Northern Railway, which transported lumber and concrete during the 20th century. The mostly crushed-stone pathway runs through cultivated fields, open space, scattered woodlands, and river bottoms. The nearby river provides for some great fishing and nice river views, as well as scenic vistas of Sauk Mountain and other Cascade Range peaks.

You can start the trail in the outskirts of Sedro-Woolley at the Fruitdale Road intersection. A portable toilet is available at the trailhead. Here, you'll have the

A herd of beefalo cattle grazes in a pasture along the trail.

County
Skagit

Endpoints
Polte Road at Coffman Ln. (Sedro-Woolley) to S. Dillard Ave. (Concrete)

Mileage
22.5

Roughness Index
2

Surface
Crushed Stone, Gravel

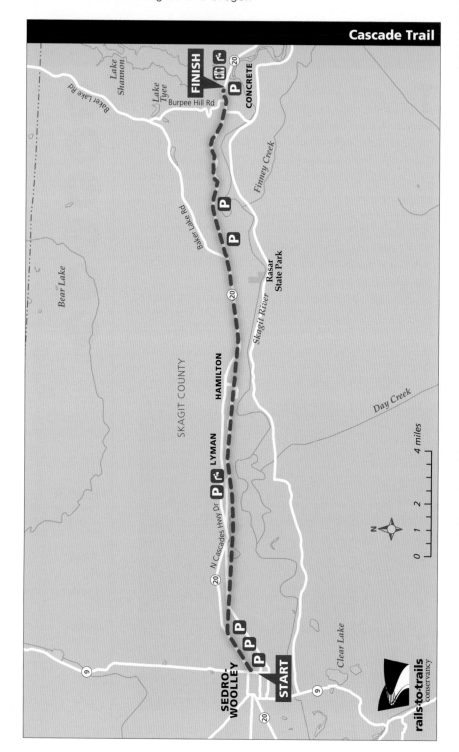

option of heading west for less than 1 mile of paved trail or east for 22 miles of crushed rock. After you've passed mile 14 and Lusk Road, consider heading south approximately 1 mile to the 169-acre Rasar State Park, a beautiful location for fishing, camping, and eagle spotting.

As you continue along the trail, note the beautiful backdrops of the region. Expect a couple detours; a little less than three-quarters of the way in, the trail diverts at Baker Lake Road onto a bridge walkway along WA 20, crosses Grandy Creek, and returns via Bird Dog Lane.

The trail ends at Concrete Senior Center (after passing concrete silos and crossing E Avenue). You'll find restrooms and water here. Cross the historic Henry Thompson Bridge, one of the longest single-span cement bridges in the West when it was built, to rest at the riverside picnic tables at the Baker River Project and Visitor Center.

CONTACT: skagitcounty.net/Departments/ParksAndRecreation/parks /cascadetrail.htm

DIRECTIONS

To access the western end of the trail, take I-5 to Exit 232/Cook Road. Head east on Cook Road for 4.3 miles. Take a left onto WA 20/WA 9, and drive 2 miles to Fruitdale Road. Turn right to the trailhead; there is easy trail access for horse trailers here.

To reach the Concrete trailhead from I-5, follow Cook Road 4.3 miles west. Turn left onto WA 20/WA 9, and follow it 23.9 miles. Turn left (north) into town on Douglas Vose III Way, and immediately turn right onto Railroad Ave. to the Concrete Senior Center.

To reach the midpoint Birdsview trailhead from Cook Road, follow WA 20 for 17.3 miles, and turn left onto Baker Lake Road. Find horse trailer parking at all trailheads.

Parking is also available in Lyman and by Challenger Road, which parallels WA 20 for 2 miles in Concrete. Skagit Transit (SKAT) stops at four points near the trail, enabling users to access shorter stretches. Find the bus schedule at **skagittransit.org/page-1412.html.**

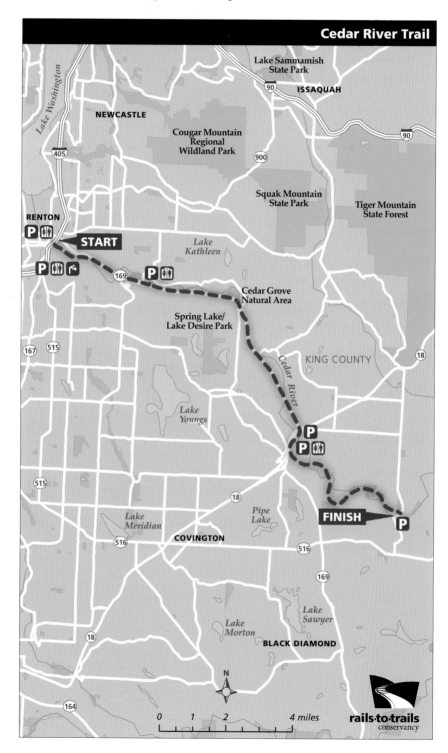

Cedar River Trail

The Cedar River Trail follows the old Chicago, Milwaukee, St. Paul and Pacific Railroad corridor on a straight, flat shot out of the sprawling Seattle metro area and into the rural countryside.

Beginning at the edge of Renton's historic downtown, the trail rolls upstream along the fast-flowing Cedar River to Landsburg Park. The first 11 miles of the trail, stretching just past the Maple Valley trailhead, are paved. There, the surface turns to packed gravel, and the path begins a winding course through a forested setting to its terminus in Landsburg, about 5 miles away.

The paved trail starts about a block from the Renton Historical Museum and passes through an open field that, a century ago, housed brick- and conduit-maker Denny-Renton Clay & Coal Co. All that remains today are

County
King

Endpoints
I-405 at Cedar River Park (Renton) to Landsburg Road SE and SE 252nd Pl. (Hobart)

Mileage
15.7

Roughness Index
1

Surface
Asphalt, Gravel

For a quick and beautiful escape from the Seattle city bustle, hop on the Cedar River Trail in Renton.

scattered bricks in the blackberry thickets. Be aware of the trail's 10-mile-per-hour bicycle speed within Renton city limits (violators face a fine up to $101); additionally, trail users on foot and wheel must stay on their side of the yellow line. After passing Ron Regis Park, the trail leaves the city limits and is sandwiched between the scenic Cedar River and busy WA 169/Maple Valley Highway. The river, filled with old snags, meanders through the valley and washes against high sandy bluffs. In the fall, you'll witness a colorful spectacle as thousands of sockeye salmon head up the river to spawn. The bright-red salmon are easily seen from trestles or the scattered county-owned natural areas that dot the river's edge. One such natural area, named Cavanaugh Pond, also is a year-round destination for spotting waterfowl. The trail becomes packed gravel after it passes the Maple Valley trailhead. This soft-surface path winds through groves of Douglas fir, western red cedar, bigleaf maple, and alder on the way to the Landsburg trailhead.

Back where the trail turns to gravel, you'll pass the 3.5-mile Green-to-Cedar Rivers Trail (not depicted on the map), another gravel rail-trail also known as the Lake Wilderness Trail. It heads up a small hill to Maple Valley's secluded Wilderness Lake and the 42-acre Lake Wilderness Arboretum. The route passes through residential Maple Valley and behind a commercial area at Kent-Kangley Road and Maple Valley Black Diamond Road/WA 169. The Green-to-Cedar Rivers Trail ends at a railroad crossing but reappears a couple of blocks later as a mountain bike, equestrian, and hiking trail in the Black Diamond Natural Area, where many paths wind through the old conifers.

CONTACT: kingcounty.gov/recreation/parks/trails.aspx

DIRECTIONS

To reach the western end, take I-405, Exit 4. From the north, the exit becomes Sunset Blvd. N. At 0.4 mile, turn right onto Bronson Way N. From the south, follow signs for WA 900/Bronson Way. After 0.3 mile on Bronson Way N, turn left onto Mill Ave. S. Proceed through an intersection with Houser Way S, and immediately turn left at a sign for CEDAR RIVER TRAIL AND CEDAR RIVER DOG PARK. Parking is on the left.

To reach the eastern end from I-405, take Exit 4. Follow WA 169 southeast for 10 miles. Turn left onto SE 216th Way, and go 3.1 miles. Turn right onto 276th Ave. SE/Landsburg Road SE, and go 2.4 miles. The trailhead is on the right, immediately before crossing Cedar River.

5 Centennial Trail State Park

Centennial Trail State Park, sometimes referred to as the Spokane River Centennial Trail, presents views of rapids and waterfalls on its 37.5-mile snaky run from the Idaho border through downtown Spokane to the rocky canyons west of town.

As its name implies, workers completed much of the on- and off-road paved trail between 1989 and 1991 during Washington State's 100-year celebration. Spokane served as a railroad crossroads, and the inactive rights-of-way and trestles of the old Spokane & Inland Empire Railroad Company and Great Northern Railway contributed to the trail corridor. Efforts continue to this day to replace road shoulder sections, and 34 of the 37.5 miles are classified as paved, off-road.

The 100-acre Riverfront Park in Spokane, designed for the Expo '74 world's fair, is the trail's midpoint centerpiece. The unique amusement park's century-old,

The city of Spokane sits along this trail and is a great place to eat, shop, or wander.

County
Spokane

Endpoints
Sontag Community Park (Nine Mile Falls) to Gateway Regional Park (Otis Orchards)

Mileage
37.5

Roughness Index
1

Surface
Asphalt

Centennial Trail State Park

hand-painted carousel blends with the urban area's natural beauty and history—reflected in bridges, dams, turn-of-the-19th-century buildings, and the old rail depot clock tower of 1902.

The downtown park is a great point to launch explorations to the east and west. The western section is more wild and rugged as it passes through Riverside State Park to the trail's end at Sontag Community Park at Nine Mile Falls. The eastern segment passes Gonzaga University and continues through a more populated region on much easier terrain. It ends at the Idaho border, where it meets the 24-mile North Idaho Centennial Trail. Drinking water, supplies, and services are limited throughout. Though the climate is hot and dry in the summer, snow and freezing temperatures are common in the wintertime.

Riverfront Park to Nine Mile Falls and Sontag Community Park: 14.8 Miles Westbound

This hilly, winding route parallels a remote section of the Spokane River. Leaving Riverfront Park, cross the North Post Street Bridge, turn left onto West Bridge Avenue, and look for the trail that heads left and passes beneath North Monroe Street and beside an overlook for Lower Falls. If you pause here long enough, you'll undoubtedly see yellow-bellied marmots scurrying among the rocks—an unusual sight in an urban area. Stay on the new section of trail past a scenic overlook to the shoulder of Summit Boulevard, and follow Summit Boulevard to Northwest Point Road on the left. Continue left onto North Pettet Drive, and then pick up the trail again to cross the river on the N. T. J. Meenach Drive Bridge. Equestrians are permitted to use the 10-mile section of trail that runs through Riverside State Park (between Sontag Community Park and the bridge).

The trail wanders through hilly terrain, young ponderosa pines, and the Riverside State Park Equestrian Area. Striking rock formations can be seen at the Bowl and Pitcher overlook. A suspension footbridge crosses the river rapids in the park for a short hike.

Back on the main trail, a basalt ridge rises overhead. Farther on, remnants of a circa 1933 Civilian Conservation Corps station can be seen at Camp Seven Mile. A brief flat section and scenic crossing of Deep Creek Bridge precedes the hills near the turbulent waters below the dam located in the Nine Mile Falls community. The trail ends just ahead at Sontag Community Park. A 1.7-mile trail extension from Sontag Community Park into the Nine Mile Recreation Area is scheduled for completion in 2015.

Riverfront Park to Idaho Border: 22.8 Miles Eastbound

This route leaves Riverfront Park by heading east past the Looff Carrousel. It crosses the Spokane River at the Don Kardong Bridge and passes through the

Gonzaga University campus. After crossing East Mission Avenue, the trail follows this serene section of river through the suburbs and into Spokane Valley along East Upriver Drive. There's a slight uphill grade as you head east along the pine-speckled, arid landscape all the way to Idaho. Parts of the trail are on the road shoulder.

Plenty of recreational activities exist along the river. Just past the Upriver Dam, the trail enters John C. Shields Park, where rock climbers hang out at an outcrop called Minnehaha Rocks. About a mile upriver is Boulder Beach; scuba divers enter the river here to explore submerged rocks.

The Centennial Trail route regains the road at Camp Sekani Park, crosses North Argonne Road, and turns right onto North Farr Road to East Maringo Drive, where the trail resumes (parking and restrooms are located here). The trail crosses the boulder-strewn river on a pedestrian bridge and enters a somewhat remote area to Mirabeau Point Park, where wildlife might be seen in the sparse forest or along the river.

The trail hugs the river as it passes Spokane Valley Mall and remains on the south shore all the way to Gateway Regional Park on the Idaho border. From here, the trail passes underneath I-90 and continues east for another 24 miles as the North Idaho Centennial Trail to Lake Coeur d'Alene.

CONTACT: spokanecentennialtrail.org

DIRECTIONS

For Riverfront Park access from I-90 W, take Exit 281, and follow S. Division St. North for 0.7 mile. Turn left onto W. Spokane Falls Blvd. From I-90 E, take Exit 280, and follow W. Fourth Ave. for 0.8 mile; then turn left onto S. Washington St. and go 0.5 mile. Look for parking in lots on the left between N. Browne and Howard Sts.

For Sontag Community Park access from I-90, take Exit 280 toward S. Walnut St. and head north for 0.5 mile. After Walnut becomes Maple St., continue another 1.4 miles, and turn left onto W. Northwest Blvd. After 0.7 mile, turn right onto N. Cochran St., which becomes N. Driscoll Blvd. At 2.6 miles, continue straight onto W. Nine Mile Road at the intersection of W. Frances Ave. Go 6.1 miles, and turn left at W. Charles St., cross the river, and continue to the park.

To reach Gateway Regional Park at the Idaho border from I-90, take Exit 299 toward the state line, and turn left onto N. Spokane Bridge Road. The park is directly ahead.

Discover Passes are required at Washington State Parks. Equestrians may park at the former stables in Riverside State Park.

The Chehalis Western Trail follows the route of a Weyerhaeuser Timber Co. railroad by the same name that carried millions of logs out of Washington forests to the coast for shipment from the 1920s to 1980s. Today, the 21.2-mile trail is the backbone for trails that link every major town in Thurston County, including the state capital, Olympia.

From the Woodard Bay Natural Resources Conservation Area (NRCA) on Puget Sound, the trail passes through forests, farms, and pastures, as well as the suburban community of Lacey, as it heads south into the hills overlooking the scenic Deschutes River valley to its intersection with the Yelm-Tenino Trail.

Users can find trailheads with parking at Woodard Bay, Chambers Lake at 14th Avenue Southeast, 67th

Serving as the backbone for Thurston County's regional trail network, the Chehalis Western Trail can be its own adventure, or it can be enjoyed in conjunction with other trails.

County
Thurston

Endpoints
Woodard Bay Natural Resources Conservation Area (Olympia) to WA 507 near the Deschutes River (Rainier)

Mileage
21.2

Roughness Index
1

Surface
Asphalt

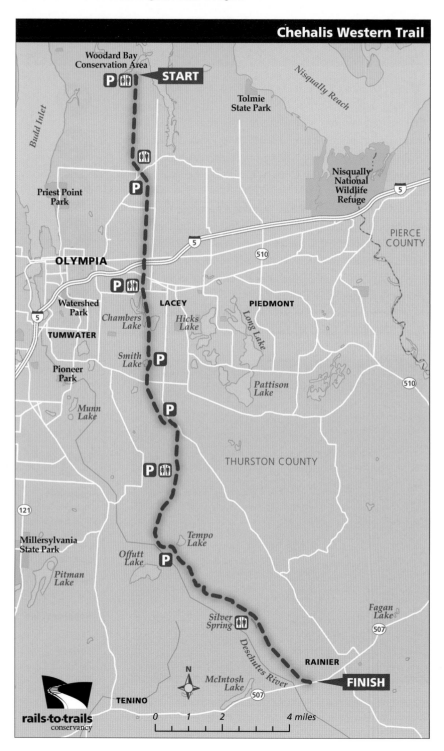

Chehalis Western Trail

Woodard Bay
Conservation Area

Tolmie
State Park

Nisqually Reach

START

Budd Inlet

Priest Point
Park

Nisqually
National
Wildlife
Refuge

PIERCE
COUNTY

OLYMPIA

Watershed
Park

LACEY

PIEDMONT

Chambers
Lake

Hicks
Lake

Long Lake

TUMWATER

Smith
Lake

Pioneer
Park

Munn
Lake

Pattison
Lake

THURSTON COUNTY

Millersylvania
State Park

Tempo
Lake

Offutt
Lake

Pitman
Lake

Silver
Spring

Fagan
Lake

RAINIER

FINISH

Deschutes River

McIntosh
Lake

TENINO

N

rails·to·trails
conservancy

0   1   2   4 miles

Avenue Southeast, and Fir Tree Road between Summerwood and Country Vista Drives Southeast. Parking spaces for two or three cars are located at several other street crossings.

If you start at the Chehalis Western Trailhead, you'll be able to hike the Upper Overlook Trail through Woodard Bay NRCA, unless you're there between April and August when the trail is closed for nesting herons. The path (hiking only) follows a siding of the former main line that crossed Woodard Bay and Weyer Point and ended at Weyerhaeuser's log dump in Chapman Bay, where logs were floated to mills in Everett. The Washington State Department of Natural Resources replanted the rail right-of-way and removed most of the trestles to restore the natural habitat here.

Heading south, you'll arrive in Lacey to find pedestrian bridges over Martin Way Southeast, I-5, and Pacific Avenue Southeast. Just south of that third bridge, the trail crosses the Woodland Trail (see page 111), which serves as a 2.5-mile connection to Olympia.

Trail traffic can get crowded in Lacey, where the old railroad corridor bisects new neighborhoods. South of town, trail users have to negotiate a short stretch of dirt trail and road shoulder to avoid an above-grade railroad crossing. After that, you'll pass the fast-flowing Deschutes River and an outdoor sculpture park before arriving at the end of the trail. There's no parking or services here, but a 2-mile ride northeast on the Yelm-Tenino Trail (see page 114) takes you to Rainier, where you'll find a small grocery, restrooms, and a restaurant.

CONTACT: co.thurston.wa.us/parks/trails-chehalis-western.htm

DIRECTIONS

To reach the Woodard Bay trailhead from I-5, take Exit 109, and head west on Martin Way SE. After 0.6 mile, turn right onto Sleater Kinney Road NE. Go 4.5 miles; the road bears left onto 56th Ave. NE. In another 0.4 mile, turn right onto Shincke Road NE; at 0.6 mile, bear left onto Woodard Bay Road NE. Parking for the trailhead is 0.4 mile ahead on the right.

To reach the Rainier Trailhead on Yelm-Tenino Trail, which connects to the Chehalis Western Trail 2 miles to the southwest, from I-5, take Exit 109, and head west on Martin Way SE. Take the first left onto College St. SE, which, in 3.7 miles, becomes Rainer Road SE after crossing Yelm Hwy. Go 9 more miles, and turn left onto 133rd Ave. SE in Rainier. In 1 mile, turn right onto Center St. N, and proceed about 0.5 mile to the trailhead.

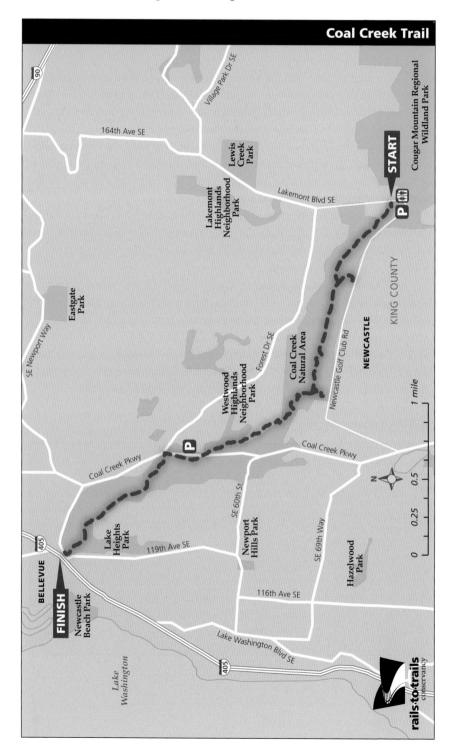

Coal Creek Trail offers trail users a wealth of coal history, fitness, and nature in a forested fish and wildlife habitat, with interpretive signs that highlight the relics to be found along the 3.7-mile soft-mulch route.

Moderate and flat terrain defines the 2.5-mile eastern segment, while continuous hills comprise the lower 1.2 miles. Boardwalks, stairs, bridges, and benches add not only safety and ease in a fairly dense forest but also artistry and impressive engineering.

From the Red Town trailhead, the trail extends into a history of coal mining beginning in the 1860s. In 1917, this multiethnic community of 1,000 people produced 360,000 tons of coal. The Seattle and Walla Walla coal trains carried their loads to the coal docks, where the coal was shipped to San Francisco. Though the rail never reached past Coal Creek, Seattle developed as a port city.

The trail begins across the street from the parking lot of Cougar Mountain Regional Wildland Park. Once inside

Evidence of the area's coal mining history, the rust-colored falls are a result of the iron salts leached from coal.

County
King

Endpoints
Red Town trailhead at Lakemont Blvd. SE and Newcastle Golf Club Road and 119th Ave. SE at I-405 (Bellevue)

Mileage
3.7

Roughness Index
2

Surface
Ballast, Dirt, Grass, Wood Chips

the deep forest, you'll find a sealed mine shaft and a short loop exposing a coal seam. The trail crosses a bridge, where a group of log benches, rust colored from the iron salts leached from coal, faces the North Fork Falls. The route continues through thick and diversely populated forest and past a cedar flume and coal bunker foundations. The narrow trail diverts from the railroad grade due to man-made hills of coal tailings (discarded rock). One mile in, if you take the 0.8-mile Primrose Trail, you'll pass the site of the old locomotive turntable. Switching back down (creek side), you'll cross three bridges before you loop back to the main trail. Wildflowers, snails, and butterflies; the tiny Sandstone Falls; and a pair of coal car axles are all visible along this part of the trail.

The main trail descends 500 feet, with occasional slippery and muddy sections. Neighborhood access trails can be found along the level creek-side section, along with a retention pond and a fish ladder (a structure that helps fish migrate around barriers). Under Coal Creek Parkway is a 1.1-mile lower trail with a fairly steep series of hills frequented by runners. You'll pass a spur up to a tiny lot at Southeast 60th Street as you reach the end at 119th Avenue Southeast.

CONTACT: tinyurl.com/coalcreektrl

DIRECTIONS

To reach the eastern endpoint, take I-90, Exit 13. Drive south on Lakemont Blvd. SE for 3.1 miles. Slow down to look for the entrance to the Red Town trailhead, located on the left side of the road at the start of a sharp curve.

The Coal Creek east trailhead is located 0.4 mile beyond Red Town, on the right.

To reach the Coal Creek Trailhead from I-405, take Exit 10, and follow Coal Creek Pkwy. SE for 1.3 miles east. Just after the light at Forest Dr., turn left into the lot. Note: No parking exists at the western endpoint of the lower trail. This section is served by a bus.

The well-maintained Cowiche Canyon Trail crosses nine bridges over Cowiche Creek on a mostly flat pathway flanked by walls of Columbia River Basalt and other rock forms. The trail is managed by the Cowiche Canyon Conservancy, which owns and maintains 2,000 acres, and manages approximately 30 miles of trails, in the Cowiche Creek and Naches River watershed areas of the Yakima Valley region. The Cowiche Canyon area is an ideal recreation site for all types of outdoor enthusiasts, including hikers, mountain bikers, runners, cross-country skiers, and wildlife observers.

Lava flowing millions of years ago, and "more recent" geological events (1 million years ago), created the floor and walls of the canyon. In 1913, the North Yakima & Valley Railway built a line to transport fruit around the region. The

County
Yakima

Endpoints
Weikel Road and
Cowiche Canyon Road
(Yakima)

Mileage
3

Roughness Index
2

Surface
Dirt, Gravel

The contrast between the lush riparian areas and the dry canyon walls provides striking landscape views along the route.

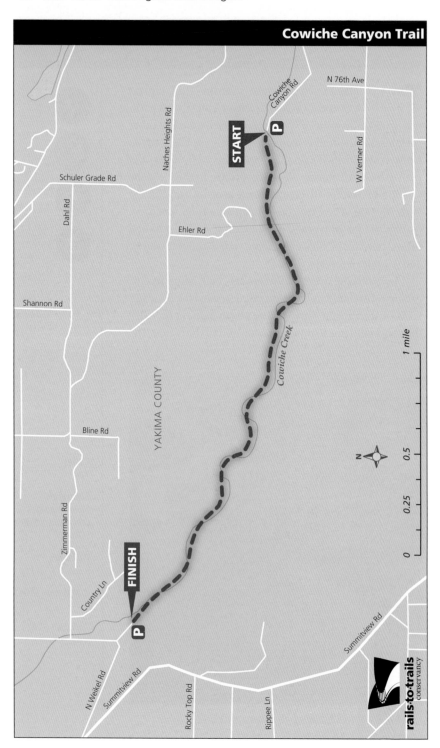

trail that inhabits this former railway climbs from the canyon floor to the top of the canyon walls, following the lush Cowiche Creek and its flora, offering glorious views and abundant habitats for birds, mammals, and aquatic life. Be sure to go in spring to witness this beauty, which is muted in summer and winter.

Along the main trail, you can branch off to several connecting trails to enjoy steeper terrain and more of the unique beauty of the area. Starting at the eastern trailhead (be sure to grab plenty of water and sunscreen) brings you quickly to bridge #9 (the first bridge of your journey). The Uplands Trail connects to the Cowiche Canyon Trail as you near bridge #8; the connecting trail climbs the south hillside and crosses the Cowiche Canyon Uplands. Here, on the plateau, you'll find another canyon access point and parking. Just west of bridge #8 is the Winery Trail; the fairly steep 0.8-mile climb leads to two tasting rooms, picnic tables, and views of Mount Adams. You can also drive to the plateau and to the wineries from two other access points. Be aware that there is a step up to some bridges, and some do not have railings. After the final bridge, you'll reach the western trailhead at Weikel Road.

CONTACT: cowichecanyon.org

DIRECTIONS

To reach the eastern Cowiche Canyon Trailhead from I-82, take Exit 31, and head west on US 12 for 3.6 miles. Turn left onto Ackley Road, and then make a fairly quick left onto W. Powerhouse Road. At 0.2 mile, turn right onto Cowiche Canyon Road. Follow the road 2.2 miles to its end to reach the trail.

To reach the Weikel trailhead from I-82, take Exit 31. Follow US 12 westbound for 2.1 miles, and take the N. 40th Ave. exit. Head south 1.5 miles to Summitview Ave., and turn right. Go 7 miles, and turn right onto N. Weikel Road. After 0.25 mile, turn right into the trailhead parking lot. Walk along the road to the kiosk and trailhead.

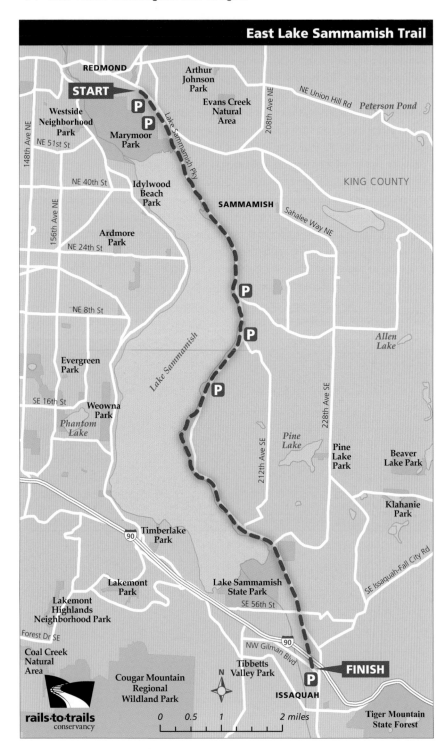

East Lake Sammamish Trail

REDMOND

Arthur Johnson Park

Evans Creek Natural Area

NE Union Hill Rd   Peterson Pond

START

Westside Neighborhood Park

NE 51st St

Marymoor Park

148th Ave NE

Lake Sammamish Pkwy

208th Ave NE

KING COUNTY

NE 40th St

Idylwood Beach Park

SAMMAMISH

Sahalee Way NE

156th Ave NE

Ardmore Park

NE 24th St

NE 8th St

Allen Lake

Evergreen Park

Lake Sammamish

SE 16th St

Weowna Park

Phantom Lake

Pine Lake

212th Ave SE

228th Ave SE

Pine Lake Park

Beaver Lake Park

Klahanie Park

Timberlake Park

90

Lakemont Park

Lakemont Highlands Neighborhood Park

Forest Dr SE

Coal Creek Natural Area

Cougar Mountain Regional Wildland Park

Lake Sammamish State Park

SE 56th St

SE Issaquah–Fall City Rd

N

Tibbetts Valley Park

NW Gilman Blvd

90

FINISH

ISSAQUAH

Tiger Mountain State Forest

rails·to·trails
conservancy

0   0.5   1   2 miles

9 East Lake Sammamish Trail

The East Lake Sammamish Trail is an important link in the Mountains to Sound Greenway, a 1.5 million–acre landscape stretching from Seattle to Central Washington. Its origins hail from the Seattle, Lake Shore and Eastern Railway, whose line along the eastern shore of Squak Lake (now Lake Sammamish) greatly aided in the development of Seattle during its brief run in the late 1800s.

Eleven miles of level trail through three suburban cities grant access to the shores of Lake Sammamish. Currently, the trail consists of a total of 6 paved miles, located at either end of the trail, with crushed rock and stone making up the middle sections (plans are under way for these sections to be paved by 2017). Trail sections are closed and paved segment by segment; however, there is a nearby parkway with a wide shoulder. Use caution, and be alert for passing vehicles.

Take a break at Sammamish Landing for a quick swim or a lakeside picnic.

County
King

Endpoints
NE 70th St. at WA 202 (Redmond) to NW Gilman Blvd. and Fourth Ave. W (Issaquah)

Mileage
11

Roughness Index
2

Surface
Crushed Stone, Asphalt

From the Northeast 70th Street lot in Redmond (adjacent to cafés and a hotel), the trail crosses several streets and a spur trail to massive Marymoor Park, home to an outdoor velodrome. The spur delivers you through the park to the Sammamish River Trail, which then links to the Burke-Gilman Trail (see page 11) stretching into Seattle. Bypassing the spur to Marymoor, head 1.2 miles along the trail to Sammamish Landing, a lovely waterfront park (with a restroom) where you can swim, fish, or stretch out on the grass. If you take the dirt track below the park gazebo, you'll find pocket beaches; you can return to the trail via a short, steep incline.

The tree-lined corridor proceeds above lakefront homes and below the mostly muffled sounds of East Lake Sammamish Parkway Northeast, with views of the hills across the lake. The paved trail gives way to a 4.8-mile journey on crushed rock. An uphill spur leads to a lot and portable restroom at mile 4.8 (destined to become the fully civilized Inglewood trailhead as development progresses). (Enjoy two grassy areas a bit farther south.) The paved trail reappears at Southeast 43rd Way as you parallel a four-lane road and commercial district. Just before the trail ends across from Gilman Village—an Issaquah retail area comprising historical homes and Issaquah Creek—you might have a clear view of the 14,410-foot Mount Rainier in the crease of the Cascade foothills. If you continue east, you'll intersect with the Issaquah-Preston Trail (see page 56).

CONTACT: kingcounty.gov/recreation/parks/trails.aspx

DIRECTIONS

To reach the Redmond trailhead from I-405, take Exit 14. Follow WA 520 eastbound for 5.5 miles, and take the WA 202/Redmond Way exit. Turn right at the light onto Redmond Way, and go 0.3 mile. Turn right at the first light, NE 70th St., and find the parking lot on the left adjacent to a shopping center.

To reach the Issaquah trailhead, take I-90 to Exit 17. Follow the ramp to the right. Head south on Front St. N, and go 0.3 mile. Turn right onto NW Gilman Blvd. After 0.3 mile, turn right onto the narrow street between the trail and the red caboose. Do not park at the boat launch at SE 43rd Way.

10 Elliott Bay Trail (Terminal 91 Bike Path)

Elliott Bay offers trail users the opportunity to enjoy art, history, and a wide variety of outdoor activities in a beautiful waterfront setting. Myrtle Edwards Park is adjacent to the Olympic Sculpture Park, Seattle Art Museum, and a public fishing pier, while Elliott Bay Marina and Smith Cove Park boast beautiful mountain views. Creative trail bridges facilitate access to city streets for recreation and commuting.

To reach the Terminal 91 Bike Path, park at Elliott Bay Marina, and head downhill past the parking lots to Smith Cove Park. Here, you'll be treated to bay views of the Ferris wheel and stadium, dwarfed by Mount Rainier. This is also the site of the once-active Northern Pacific coal bunker pier—a 2,500-foot trestle constructed in 1891—replaced in 1899 by Great Northern Railroad Piers 88 and 89. In 1921, the Port of Seattle built Piers 40 and 41 (later renumbered to 90 and 91), which—at 2,530 feet—were acknowledged to be the longest concrete piers in the world.

Signs direct you toward a fenced pathway and past 20th Avenue West, which leads to the Ballard Locks.

Art is scattered along this urban waterfront trail.

County
King

Endpoints
Myrtle Edwards Park at Broad St. to Elliott Bay Marina at Smith Cove Park (Seattle)

Mileage
3.4

Roughness Index
1

Surface
Asphalt

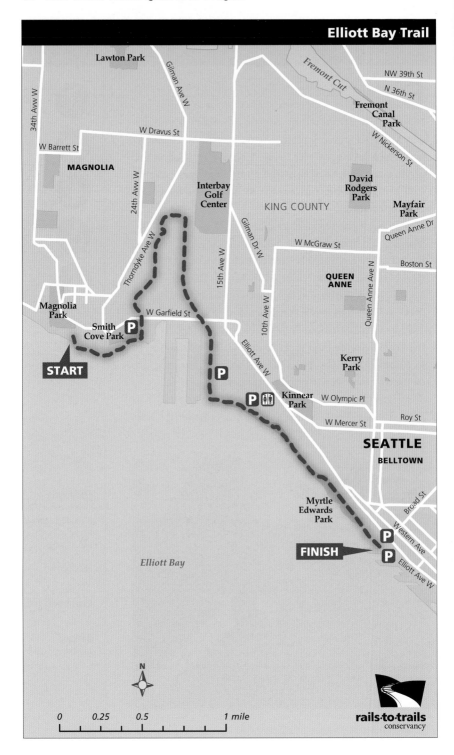

Elliott Bay Trail

Lawton Park

Gilman Ave W

NW 39th St

N 36th St

Fremont Cut

34th Avw W

W Dravus St

Fremont
Canal
Park

W Nickerson St

W Barrett St

MAGNOLIA

24th Avw W

Interbay
Golf
Center

KING COUNTY

David
Rodgers
Park

Mayfair
Park

Queen Anne Dr

Thorndyke Ave W

15th Ave W

Gilman Dr W

W McGraw St

Boston St

**QUEEN
ANNE**

Queen Anne Ave N

Magnolia
Park

W Garfield St

10th Ave W

Smith
Cove Park

P

Elliott Ave W

Kerry
Park

START

P

W Olympic Pl

Roy St

P

Kinnear
Park

W Mercer St

SEATTLE

BELLTOWN

Myrtle
Edwards
Park

Broad St

Western Ave

FINISH

P

P

Elliott Ave W

Elliott Bay

N

0   0.25   0.5   1 mile

rails·to·trails
conservancy

Beside active BNSF Railway tracks, a steep overpass suggests walking your bike or sidestepping your skates down the very narrow descent. After crossing a set of tracks, you'll arrive at the civilized and scenic trail beside the West Galer Street parking area at 1.75 miles. (Park here to avoid the Terminal 91 section.)

Once in Myrtle Edwards Park, you'll pass a public fishing pier and a grain terminal. A grassy area with benches and landscape art separates pedestrian and wheeled paths. Beginner skaters can expect a bit of buckled pavement and a few curves. An impressive bridge rises above the park to a Puget Sound viewpoint before the trail exits by stairway to Elliott Avenue West and by ramp to Third Avenue West, with a signed route to Seattle Center. The bayside rocks, benches, and grassy areas invite a break before you reach Olympic Sculpture Park.

Exit to the sidewalk or the trail on the east side of Alaskan Way to enjoy summer concerts, the Ferris wheel, an aquarium, Pike Place Market, Pioneer Square, and the ferries. The Seattle waterfront redesign begins in 2016 and will include open space and nonmotorized pathways along the waterfront.

CONTACT: seattle.gov/transportation/urbantrails.htm

DIRECTIONS

On-street parking can be found at the southern trail endpoint if you're willing to search a bit and walk or cycle to the park. Busing here with a bike and to other pedestrian/bike access points is common.

Three pedestrian/bike bridges access the western side of the trail from Elliott Ave. Turn west off Elliott Ave. on Galer St., and walk up steps to a separated roadside trail over the BNSF tracks. Steps and a sidewalk descend to the road and under the bridge to the well-signed trail sites. An additional pedestrian/bike bridge with an elevator crosses the tracks here, closer to the fishing pier, to land on W. Prospect St. at Elliott Ave. The third bridge, described above, crosses from the south end of Myrtle Edwards Park and reaches W. Thomas St. for pedestrians and Third Ave. W on a cyclist ramp.

To reach Elliott Bay Marina from I-5, take Exit 167 (W. Mercer St.). Go 1.6 miles, and turn right onto Elliott Ave. W. At 0.6 mile, turn left onto W. Garfield St. (follow the Magnolia Bridge signs). Stay in the right lane, and take the first exit to the right (follow signs for the Cruise Terminal and Elliott Bay Marina). At the bottom of the ramp, turn left. Park at the STREET END sign. Only permit parking is allowed in the lots unless you are dining at a restaurant.

To reach the parking area across from Pier 90, follow the directions above to Elliott Ave. W, and turn right. In 0.4 mile, follow the EXIT ONLY signs for Terminals 86–91 and the Magnolia Bridge. Once you turn right, immediately bear left; the bridge will carry you over Elliott Ave. At the end of the bridge, turn right onto Alaskan Way, and then turn right onto W. Galer St. Parking is available along the trail.

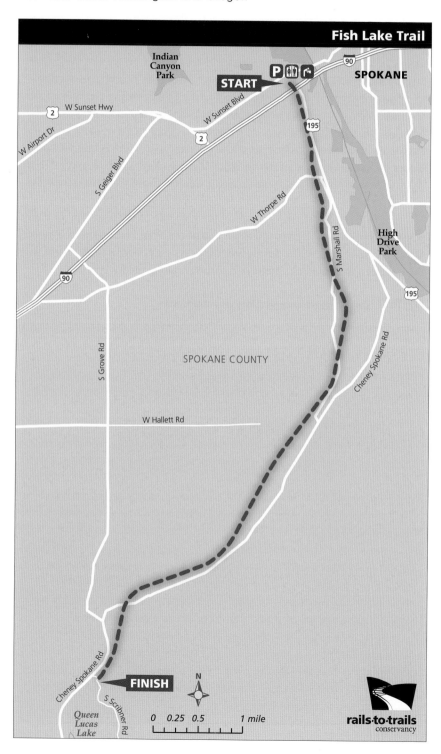

Fish Lake Trail

The Fish Lake Trail leaves West Spokane and runs south through open forest to reach Queen Lucas Lake, which is 1.5 miles north of the trail's ultimate planned destination, Fish Lake Regional Park. Upon completion of this gap, two bridges over active rail lines will join this trail to 3.5 paved miles of the Columbia Plateau Trail, serving as a corridor for commuting and recreation between Spokane and the college town of Cheney.

From the Spokane trailhead, the route follows a mild uphill grade; to your left, trees separate you from US 195 for a couple miles and then from Cheney Spokane Road, which loosely parallels the trail. Half-mile markers guide you through the hot, dry uplands of Eastern Washington.

The trail follows a piece of corridor of the Oregon-Washington Railroad & Navigation Company (a division of the Union Pacific Railroad) through the Latah Valley, formerly Hangman Valley. At Marshall Canyon, take in

County
Spokane

Endpoints
Milton St. trailhead to Queen Lucas Lake (Spokane)

Mileage
9

Roughness Index
1

Surface
Asphalt

The Fish Lake Trail showcases some fantastic railroad settings, including "The Funnel" of Marshall Canyon.

railroad history as you travel beside active rail lines through the area known by railfans as "The Funnel."

The Scribner Road trailhead offers access to scenic Queen Lucas Lake. Experienced commuters might leave the trail at South Scribner Road to continue 2 miles to Fish Lake, where the wide shoulders of the two-lane Cheney Spokane Road and the Columbia Plateau Trail offer separate routes to Cheney (and Eastern Washington University). Just farther south, the Columbia Plateau Trail leads into the Turnbull National Wildlife Refuge; a hard-packed dirt and gravel surface, which becomes less passable mid-trail, replaces the paved trail just before reaching the refuge.

Future plans bridge a short gap on city roads to link the Fish Lake Trail to Centennial Trail State Park (see page 21).

CONTACT: inlandnorthwesttrails.org/projects/fish_lake_trail.asp

DIRECTIONS

To reach the Spokane trailhead, take I-90 to Exit 279. Continue on US 195 S for 0.3 mile. Turn right onto W. 16th Ave., which becomes S. Lindeke St. and curves to the right. In 0.6 mile, turn right to stay on S. Lindeke St. (which becomes S. Milton St.), and then make an immediate right into the trailhead parking lot.

To reach the Scribner Road trailhead, take I-90 to Exit 270. Turn left onto W. Melville Road, and go 4 miles. Turn right onto S. Spotted Road, and in 0.7 mile, turn left onto W. Andrus Road. In 0.8 mile, turn right onto S. Grove Road, and then take a right onto Cheney Spokane Road. In 0.6 mile, take a left onto S. Scribner Road, and you will see a small gravel lot on your right.

The Foothills Trail is a 30-mile collection of six unconnected segments of the old Burlington Northern Railway that served the farming, coal-mining, and logging economies near the base of Mount Rainier.

The longest section is a paved trail that rolls for 15.1 miles between the outskirts of Puyallup to South Prairie. Other paved, gravel, and dirt segments are located in Enumclaw, Buckley, and Wilkeson, as well as an isolated 1.3-mile asphalt trail with four bridges in an area known as Cascade Junction. Plans call for connecting all these pieces.

The Northern Pacific Railway Company laid its tracks from Tacoma to the coalfields around Wilkeson in 1877. In 1970, the railroad merged into Burlington Northern, which ceased using the lines in 1982. Two years later, residents began working to create the Foothills Trail.

Running along the foothills of Mount Rainier, this trail offers breathtaking views of the iconic volcano at various points along the way.

Counties
King, Pierce

Endpoints
Pioneer Way E and 134th Ave. E (Puyallup) to Pioneer Way E/WA 162 and Cross Creek Ct. (South Prairie); 132nd Ave. E to just past WA 410 and Cemetery Road at Boise Creek (Buckley); SE 416th St. near Veazie-Cumberland Road SE to Washington Ave. and First St. (Enumclaw); Veteran's Memorial Park at WA 410 and Mountain Villa Dr. to SE Mud Mountain Road near the White River (Enumclaw); 156th St. Ct. E at 272nd Ave. E (Wilkeson) to 268th Ave. E at 146th St. E (South Prairie); Pearl St. Ct. at WA 165/Church St. (Wilkeson) to WA 165 and Pershing Ave. (Carbonado)

Mileage
30

Roughness Index
1

Surface
Asphalt, Gravel, Dirt

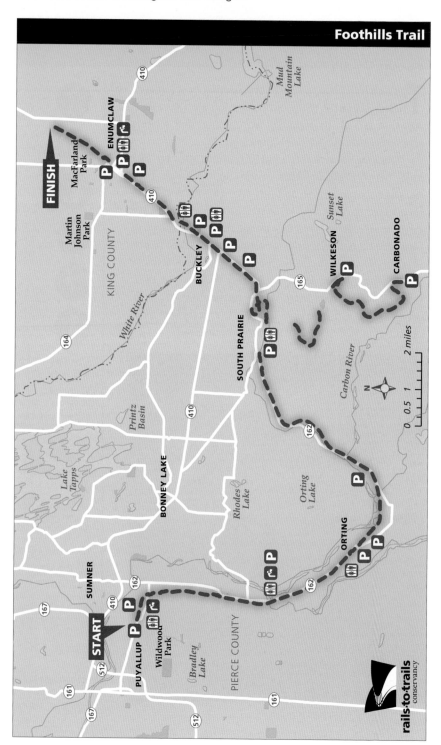

Foothills Trail

Puyallup to South Prairie

The most popular trail is the Puyallup-South Prairie piece. It boasts four trail-heads along the route at East Puyallup, McMillin, Orting, and South Prairie, in addition to other parking.

Here, you'll pass through farmland that once produced 60 million daffodil bulbs annually. All that remains of that era is the annual Daffodil Festival, as well as that bloom's depictions on signs and even a sculpture along the route. About halfway, the town of Orting offers a bike shop, cafés, bakeries, and more.

Later, the trail crosses the Carbon River that runs milky white from a melting glacier on Mount Rainier. The active volcano's white summit is visible most of the way. It's responsible for making this perhaps the only rail-trail posted with lahar warning signs, which direct trail users to head for the hills to escape volcanic mudflow in the event of seismic activity.

A picnic shelter set up by a local roadside coffee stand welcomes trail users to the endpoint in South Prairie. Pierce County acquired a piece of right-of-way here in 2013 that can be used to extend the trail through to Cascade Junction (an old railroad landmark), thus joining the main trail to branches in Buckley and Wilkeson.

Buckley to Cascade Junction

A 2.4-mile paved section of the Foothills Trail starts at the White River at the north end of Buckley. It passes the stadium for the annual logging contests and a historical display of log-industry artifacts. The pavement ends at a USE AT OWN RISK sign south of town. Those who venture ahead through ankle-deep mud will come to the old railroad S-curve built to reach the elevation of the Enumclaw Plateau in less than 1.5 miles. Despite the four bridges (one 400 feet long) and 1.3 miles of paved surface, this area is rarely visited because of its difficult access. Additionally, as of spring 2015, bridge damage on the trail segment's northern end has made access even more difficult. This segment ends at a gate just short of Cascade Junction. Do not use the private road in this area.

Wilkeson to Carbonado

Wilkeson, with its old-timey Main Street storefronts, is one of the few surviving towns from the coal-mining era. A 1-mile-long paved trail takes a switchback uphill to a well-maintained dirt singletrack that completes the 4.4-mile journey through the woods to historic Carbonado. Future plans call for pushing the dirt trail past at least one ghost town along the former rail line.

North of town, another singletrack starts at an unmarked trailhead on the left side of 156th Street Court East, about 200 feet west of the intersection with Johns Road East. The dirt trail heads through the narrow valley formed by

Wilkeson Creek. With the future development of the Cascade Junction gap, trail users can connect to South Prairie or Buckley.

Enumclaw

Two more Foothills Trail sections start in Enumclaw, located in southern King County. One heads north into farmland for 1.9 miles. This starts as a 0.2-mile paved trail and then becomes gravel and later a dirt track running between pasture fence lines. The 2.1-mile southern segment starts east of downtown and heads south toward Buckley on asphalt for 1.2 miles. A soft surface follows, but that becomes impassable before SE Mud Mountain Road. A pedestrian bridge across the White River between Enumclaw and Buckley is just one of many projects being considered for the Foothills Trail.

CONTACT: piercecountytrails.org

DIRECTIONS

To reach the East Puyallup trailhead, from the intersection of WA 167 and WA 410 in Sumner, follow WA 410 E for 1.3 miles. Take the WA 162/Valley Ave. exit toward Orting, and follow WA 162 for 0.5 mile south. Turn right onto 80th St. E. The East Puyallup trailhead is about 1 mile ahead on the right.

To reach the South Prairie trailhead, from the intersection of WA 167 and WA 410 near Sumner, follow WA 410 E. After 5.7 miles, turn right onto S. Prairie Road E. In 4.1 miles, turn right onto Pioneer Way E and look for the South Prairie trailhead sign.

For Buckley access, from the intersection of WA 167 and WA 410 near Sumner, follow WA 410 toward Yakima. After 12.5 miles, you'll arrive in Buckley. Turn right onto Park Ave., and then turn left onto N. River Road. Look for Buckley Log Show parking on the left.

For the closest access to Cascade Junction, from the intersection of WA 167 and WA 410 near Sumner, follow WA 410 toward Yakima. Go 11.8 miles, and bear right onto WA 165/S. River Road. Look for a gravel parking lot on the right in about 1 mile.

For Wilkeson access, from the intersection of WA 167 and WA 410 near Sumner, follow WA 410 toward Yakima. After 10.7 miles, turn right onto Mundy Loss Road. In 1.2 miles, turn left onto WA 162, and then turn right onto WA 165. Follow WA 165 2.8 miles to the Wilkeson welcome arch, and look for the parking lot on the right.

For Carbonado access, from the intersection of WA 167 and WA 410 near Sumner, follow WA 410 toward Yakima. After 10.7 miles, turn right onto Mundy Loss Road. In 1.2 miles, turn left onto WA 162, and then turn right onto WA 165. Follow WA 165 for 5.1 miles to Pershing Ave. on the right.

For Enumclaw access from I-405 in Renton, take Exit 4 onto WA 169 toward Maple Valley. Follow WA 169 S for 25.5 miles, and turn left onto WA 164/Griffin Ave. in Enumclaw. In three blocks, turn right onto Railroad St. Public parking is available on either side of the road.

Spectacular views across Bellingham Bay to the San Juan Islands and beyond reward visitors of this Interurban Trail. All they have to do is find a clearing along the wooded path that runs a fairly level course across the Chuckanut Mountains between the historic Fairhaven community and Larrabee State Park.

The mostly packed gravel and dirt trail combines the corridors of two former railroads that serviced the area before reliable roads were built in the Pacific Northwest. The longest segment follows the Bellingham & Skagit Interurban Railway, an electric trolley that ran passengers and freight from Bellingham to Mount Vernon from 1912 to 1930. Another trail section in the north follows the railbed of the Fairhaven & Southern Railroad that ran coal trains to and from Sedro-Woolley in the late 1800s

Along the forested sections of this trail are many clearings with sweeping views of the Puget Sound.

County
Whatcom

Endpoints
Donovan Ave. at 10th St. (Fairhaven) to Larrabee State Park at Fragrance Lake Road and Chuckanut Dr. (Bellingham)

Mileage
6.7

Roughness Index
2

Surface
Crushed Stone, Dirt

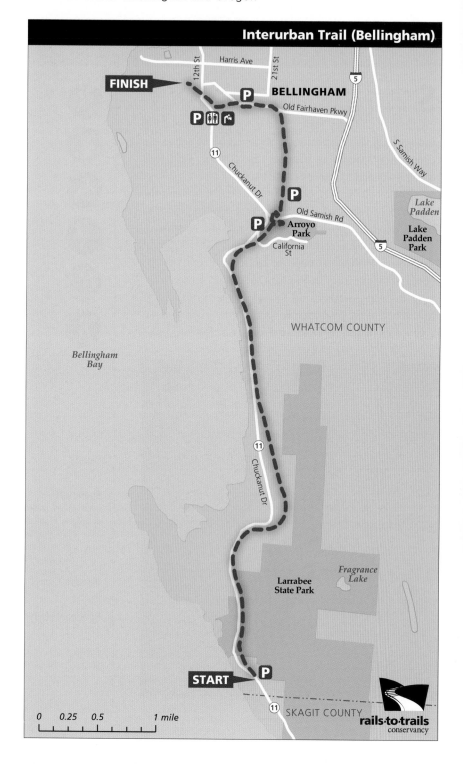

Interurban Trail (Bellingham)

FINISH

Harris Ave

12th St

21st St

5

BELLINGHAM

Old Fairhaven Pkwy

S Samish Way

11

Chuckanut Dr

Old Samish Rd

Lake Padden

Arroyo Park

Lake Padden Park

California St

5

WHATCOM COUNTY

Bellingham Bay

11

Chuckanut Dr

Fragrance Lake

Larrabee State Park

START

11   SKAGIT COUNTY

0   0.25   0.5   1 mile

rails·to·trails
conservancy

through the turn of the 19th century. At the southern end, the route starts at the Clayton Beach trailhead in Larrabee State Park. The state park was the first in Washington, created with a donation of 20 acres by the Larrabee family in 1915. Several foot trails cross the forested park, but the Interurban leaves from the northwest corner of the clearing. A second-growth forest shades the gentle path for a couple miles until an opening offers vistas to the west that stop many travelers in their tracks.

After passing a waterfall, visitors are faced with a decision at the California Street crossing, about 4 miles from the Clayton Beach trailhead. A missing railroad trestle across a deep canyon formed by Chuckanut Creek means either traveling a mile by road or taking 0.75 mile of steep singletrack through Arroyo Park. Prudent travelers turn left onto California Street, right onto Chuckanut Drive, and right again at a trail sign at Old Samish Road. Even so, they have a couple of switchbacks to tackle on the groomed gravel trail that returns to the railroad grade.

Those on foot or with good bike-handling skills can dive into the steep narrow trail across California Street and take the right fork. Entering a mossy forest that echoes with babbling Chuckanut Creek, they emerge at a long wooden bridge. Two left forks lead to the Old Samish Road crossing and a return to the groomed trail. A spur trail up here reveals pilings from the missing 500-foot trestle reincarnated as a bench.

Approaching the fringes of Fairhaven (now part of Bellingham), the trail crosses 20th Street to follow the sidewalk beside Julia Avenue for a short distance, passing the Rotary Club trailhead. The trail forks to the right at 18th Street and follows the Padden Creek Greenway to the end at 10th Street and Donovan Avenue. The Lower Padden Trail continues to the waterfront along Bellingham Bay.

CONTACT: cob.org/services/recreation/parks-trails/trail-guide.aspx

DIRECTIONS

To reach the Clayton Beach trailhead, take I-5 to Exit 250, and travel west approximately 1.5 miles on Old Fairhaven Pkwy./WA 11. Turn left onto 12th St., and then bear left onto Chuckanut Dr./WA 11. After 5 miles, turn left into the Clayton Beach trailhead parking lot at Larrabee State Park. A Discover Pass is required to park here.

To reach the Rotary trailhead (Fairhaven), take I-5 to Exit 250, and travel west on Old Fairhaven Pkwy./WA 11. Look for the Rotary trailhead on the left in approximately 0.9 mile, just past 20th St. (The Fairhaven endpoint is 0.6 mile west on the trail.)

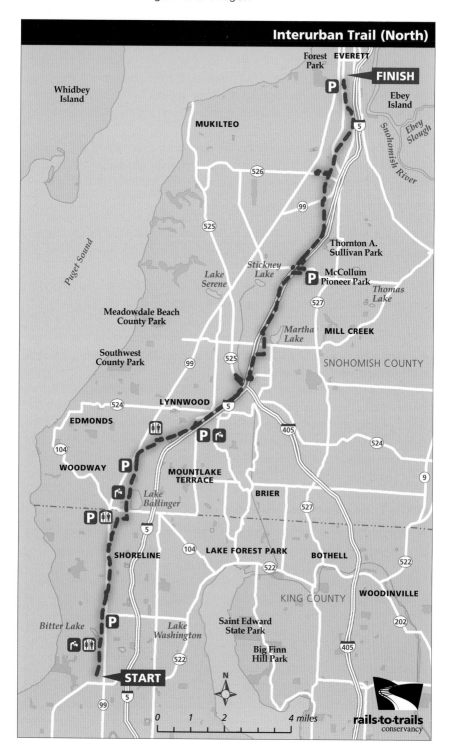

Interurban Trail (North)

14 Interurban Trail (North)

The Interurban Trail between Seattle and Everett stitches together a dense residential and commercial patchwork that the original electric railway helped to grow in the early part of the 20th century. The 24-mile trail also goes through the communities of Shoreline, Mountlake Terrace, Edmonds, and Lynnwood. It skirts two regional malls (Alderwood and Everett), a casino, and an abandoned drive-in theater, among other businesses.

The corridor for the Seattle-Everett Traction Company was considered remote when it launched service in 1910. As growth mushroomed after World War I, commuter and mercantile traffic switched to cars and trucks on new roads, and the railway (then owned by Puget Sound Power & Light Company) folded in 1939. Snohomish County, Lynnwood, and Everett pooled their resources to create the first 11.8 miles of trail in the mid-1990s. More trail gaps are closed every few years.

The rail-trail is a 10- to 12-foot-wide paved path that travels through park or greenbelt settings. Several long sections roll adjacent to noisy I-5, which took the place of

The connection between Seattle and Everett, and the communities in between, makes this trail ideal for active commutes.

Counties
King, Snohomish

Endpoints
N. 110th St. and Fremont Ave. N (Seattle) to 41st St. and Broadway just west of I-5 (Everett)

Mileage
24

Roughness Index
1

Surface
Asphalt

the railway corridor. Anyone traveling the entire distance, however, will stumble across a dozen gaps where the marked Interurban Trail detours onto bike lanes, wide shoulders, low-traffic streets, and sidewalks.

Starting in northwest Seattle, you'll pass several examples of trailside art, including some depicting a volcano erupting, an elk sprouting horns, and other scenes in a series of sequential signs. The trail section ends at a two-way cycle track on Linden Avenue with automatic crossing signals for bicycles.

The trail resumes through the commercial center of Shoreline and ends at picturesque Echo Lake. From here, it follows a 1-mile detour onto bike lanes and a path to the Lake Ballinger Station trailhead, which features a historical exhibit of the railway. As with all trail detours, look for the distinctive Interurban Trail signs showing a red arrow on a green circle on either a white or brown background.

Heading north, you'll encounter other trail gaps, often at major intersections. Some pedestrian crossings offer scenic views of peaks in the Cascade Range to the east. One trailside curiosity south of Everett Mall is the abandoned Puget Park Drive-In, which featured its last picture show in 2009. The trail ends on a sidewalk at the busy intersection of Colby Avenue and 41st Street in Everett.

CONTACT: seattle.gov/transportation/interurbantrail.htm

DIRECTIONS

To access the trail in Seattle, from I-5, take Exit 173. If coming from the south, turn left onto First Ave. NE. Head west on N. Northgate Way, which becomes N. 105th St., for 1.1 miles. Turn right onto N. Park Ave. N, and go 0.2 mile. Turn left onto N. 110th St. Find on-street parking.

To reach the Everett trailhead, from I-5, take Exit 192, and head west on 41st St. Go one block, and turn left onto Colby Ave. After 0.3 mile, turn left onto 44th St. SE. Find a small parking lot on the right.

The Interurban Trail (South) connects several towns south of Seattle along the historic route of the Puget Sound Electric Railway. The trolley ran between Tacoma and Seattle from 1902 to 1928, falling victim to the growing popularity of cars and trucks and the construction of WA 99. Its cousin—now the Interurban Trail (North) (see page 50)—ran between Seattle and Everett and survived until 1939.

The 18.1-mile trail runs nearly straight and flat for 14.8 miles from its beginning in the north near Fort Dent Park. The route connects the towns of Tukwila, Kent, Auburn, Algona, and Pacific, making it popular with commuting bicyclists. Two unattached segments in Edgewood and Milton follow the old railway corridor toward Tacoma.

Starting at the parking lot at Fort Dent Park, follow the RIVER TRAIL signs across a small bridge, and take the Green

Portions of the trail are as straight as an arrow, reflective of the rail corridor on which it is built.

Counties
King, Pierce

Endpoints
Green River Trail at Fort Dent Way (Tukwila) to 70th Ave. E (Fife)

Mileage
18.1

Roughness Index
1

Surface
Asphalt

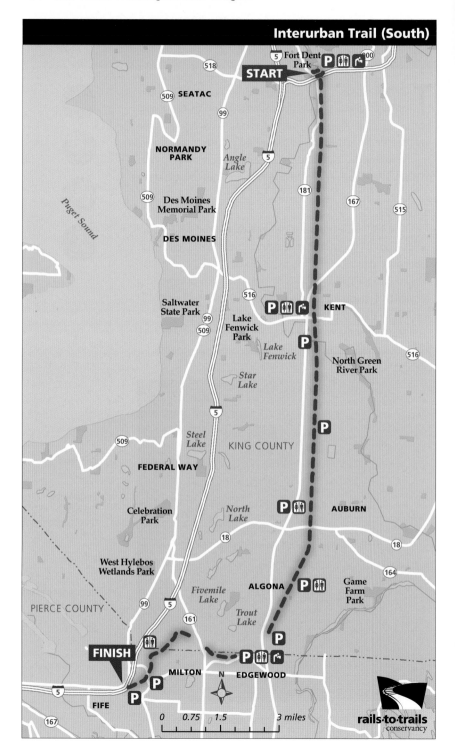

River Trail to the Interurban Trail intersection. After crossing under I-405, the paved trail rolls alongside the BNSF Railway and beneath Puget Sound Energy power lines on steel utility poles that march south for miles. The route passes sprawling commercial and light industrial areas in Tukwila and Kent with access to employers and shopping malls, though the trail avoids the hustle and bustle of the congested roads. Drainage ditches account for natural habitat next to the trail and provide nesting for ducks and marsh birds. On clear days, 14,410-foot Mount Rainier is visible to the south. After passing the outskirts of downtown Kent, the Interurban Trail meets the Green River Trail again. Following this path to the right provides a winding, 11-mile scenic route back to Fort Dent atop a river levee.

The surroundings become more agricultural after a rail yard (watch for unmanned locomotives), and you might hear a crowd roaring as you pass the Emerald Downs thoroughbred racetrack. The trail passes historic downtown Auburn and then takes its one turn, a slight curve heading to the southwest toward Tacoma. The trail passes backyards in Algona before it ends in Pacific.

The Interurban Trail segments along the ridge look nothing like the older stretch in the flatland. One 0.8-mile section begins at the Jovita Crossroads Trailhead Park in Edgewood, where you'll find a historical railway display. After another gap, the 2.5-mile Milton section descends toward Tacoma through the forested canyon of Hylebos Creek. Long-range plans call for linking the segments, though trail builders will have to find a route up the hogback from the town of Pacific, the former home of the railway's Bluffs Station.

CONTACT: kingcounty.gov/recreation/parks/trails.aspx

DIRECTIONS

To the Tukwila trailhead, from I-5, take Exit 156, and head southeast on Interurban Ave. S. Go 1.7 miles, and turn left onto Fort Dent Way. Then, turn left onto Starfire Way. From I-405, take Exit 1, and go straight across Interurban Ave. (heading north) to Fort Dent Way. Turn left onto Starfire Way.

To the Pacific trailhead, from I-5, take Exit 142A. Head east on WA 18 for 2.5 miles, and take the W. Valley Hwy. exit toward WA 167 S. Turn right onto W. Valley Hwy., and go 2.6 miles. Turn left onto Third Ave. SW. The trailhead is on the left after passing under WA 167.

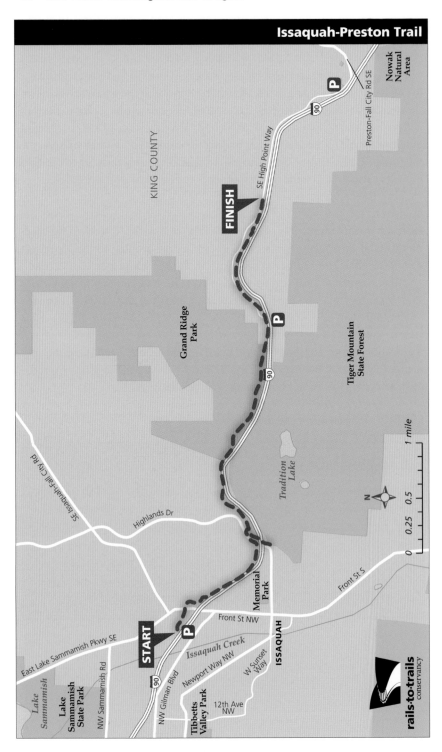

16 Issaquah-Preston Trail

Suburban sprawl gives way to deep forest and rural farm lots as this rail-trail follows an uphill grade from Issaquah to the outskirts of Preston. The Issaquah-Preston Trail is among a group of trails in the Mountains to Sound Greenway that link Seattle and its eastern suburbs with Eastern Washington. It roughly follows the original route of the Seattle, Lake Shore and Eastern Railway that was purchased by Northern Pacific at the close of the 19th century and was completely inactive by the early 1980s.

The Issaquah-Preston Trail begins at a junction with the East Lake Sammamish Trail, about 0.2 mile north of the latter trail's Issaquah endpoint. Starting as a paved trail, the Issaquah-Preston Trail crosses East Lake Sammamish Parkway at a crosswalk and traffic light and then proceeds uphill, where its role as a commuter and recreation route is evident. To reach Preston, you'll follow the

County
King

Endpoints
Fourth Ave. NW (Issaquah) to SE High Point Way (Preston)

Mileage
4.8

Roughness Index
2

Surface
Asphalt, Gravel

Decades after the last trains came through, bikers and hikers now propel themselves along this old Northern Pacific corridor.

left fork at a trail junction and enter a short tunnel; the right fork ascends to homes, stores, and offices in the Issaquah Highlands development. Another trail junction confronts visitors after the tunnel. The left branch proceeds to Preston, while the right heads downhill to historic downtown Issaquah. The paved surface ends after the second trail fork, and the subsequent packed dirt and gravel trail can be uneven and muddy at times. It becomes a wide forest path canopied by second-growth Douglas firs and western red cedars as it passes through a section of Grand Ridge Park while noisy I-90 traffic rolls past downhill. Nearly 10 miles of popular mountain biking trails in the 1,300-acre forest can be reached from the Coal Mine and Grand Ridge trailheads (maps are displayed on posts) in this section.

Passing through the forest, the path crosses a classic wooden bridge over East Fork Issaquah Creek and emerges at a small parking lot on Southeast High Point Way. Across this road, the trail continues as a gravel path sandwiched between Issaquah Creek and I-90. It is screened from the freeway by landscaping in places, and visitors can glimpse some farm lots to the north.

The Issaquah-Preston Trail ends as it crosses another wooden bridge and arrives at a two-way cycle track on the wide shoulder of Southeast High Point Way. The historic mill and railroad town of Preston—with restrooms, a market, a sports park, and the Preston-Snoqualmie Trail (see page 83)—is located about a mile to the east along the marked bike route.

CONTACT: kingcounty.gov/recreation/parks/trails.aspx or **mtsgreenway.org**

DIRECTIONS

To reach the Issaquah trailhead, take I-90 to Exit 17. Head south on Front St. N, and turn right onto NW Gilman Blvd. In 0.3 mile, turn right onto an unnamed narrow street between the East Lake Sammamish Trail and a red caboose. You can park adjacent to the Issaquah-Preston Trail 0.2 mile ahead, on the street.

To reach the Preston-Snoqualmie trailhead, take I-90 to Exit 22. Head east on SE 82nd St., and turn right at the T onto SE High Point Way. Go two blocks, and turn left onto SE 87th Pl. A parking lot is on the left. The trail is 1.5 miles west via the Preston-Snoqualmie Trail and SE High Point Way.

To reach the SE High Point Way parking lot, take I-90 to Exit 20. Head east on SE High Point Way for 1.5 miles, and look for the lot on the right.

17 John Wayne Pioneer Trail (Milwaukee Road Corridor)

Spanning an estimated 253 miles, the John Wayne Pioneer Trail is the longest rail-trail conversion in the United States. Much of it is so remote and desolate, however, that weeks will pass in some sections where the only visitors are coyotes, black-tailed jackrabbits, or gopher snakes.

Anyone traveling the entire length of the trail will experience many landscapes: mountains, dense forests, irrigated farmland, arid scrubland, and the rolling hills of the Palouse region. The route crosses the Cascade Mountains in a 2.3-mile-long, unlit tunnel and traverses numerous canyons and rivers via bridges and trestles that offer spectacular views.

The trail follows the corridor of the Chicago, Milwaukee, St. Paul & Pacific Railroad, also known as the Milwaukee Road. Workers completed the railroad's rugged

The impressive trestles on the John Wayne Pioneer Trail are reason enough to make the trip.

Counties
Adams, Grant, King, Kittitas, Spokane, Whitman

Endpoints
Rattlesnake Lake to Washington–Idaho border north of Tekoa

Mileage
253

Roughness Index
2

Surface
Crushed Stone, Ballast, Sand

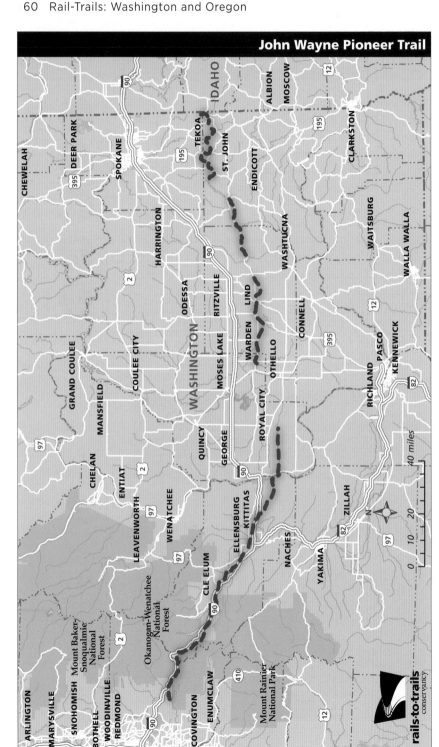

John Wayne Pioneer Trail

western mainline that connected Chicago with Seattle and Tacoma in 1909. By 1980, the railroad had ceased operations on the right-of-way. The state acquired most of the corridor and named it for John Wayne after a lobbying campaign by outdoorsman Chic Hollenbeck, a big fan of the cowboy actor. Hollenbeck also founded the John Wayne Pioneer Wagons and Riders Association, whose members make an annual trek along the trail by wagon and horseback.

The western segment of the John Wayne Pioneer Trail between Cedar Falls and the Columbia River runs through Iron Horse State Park, a 110-mile-long linear park. The Washington State Department of Natural Resources (DNR) manages the trail between the Columbia River and Lind, and the remainder from Lind to the Idaho border falls once again to the oversight of Washington State Parks.

Through most of Iron Horse State Park, the trail surface comprises well-packed crushed rock, except for the 20 miles of loose sand in the U.S. Army Yakima Training Center. Note: As of 2015, this section of trail between the Army West trailhead near Kittitas and the Army East trailhead near the Columbia River was closed due to damage incurred during a wildlands fire in mid-July 2014.

The trail is mostly track ballast east of the Columbia River. Four trailside primitive campsites are available: two between Cedar Falls and Hyak and two between Hyak and Easton.

State trailheads are located at Cedar Falls, Twin Falls, Hyak, Easton, South Cle Elum, Thorp, Ellensburg West, Ellensburg East, Kittitas, Army West, and Army East. East of the Columbia River, trailheads are planned at Malden, Rosalia, Pandora, and Tekoa.

The westernmost trailhead is nestled in the Cascade foothills, just 35 miles from downtown Seattle. Beginning near the old Cedar Falls train stop, this 22-mile uphill railroad grade gets the most visitors. The trail crosses a half-dozen canyons on trestles with sweeping mountain vistas and bores through the 100-year-old tunnel at Snoqualmie Pass to Hyak. Some bicyclists shuttle between Cedar Falls and Hyak to take advantage of a downhill run.

The eastern slope of the Cascades contains sparser vegetation—a product of the dryer climate on this side of the mountains. The trail skirts two lakes—Keechelus and Easton—that store irrigation water for the region. Later, the trail descends the secluded Upper Yakima Canyon, where pedestrians must sign a waiver to enter two tunnels.

The old railroad yard in South Cle Elum, a National Historic Landmark, preserves the history of the Milwaukee Road corridor through a surviving depot and electric substation, as well as through descriptions of the foundations of other buildings.

The trail breaks briefly at historic Ellensburg, which is the largest town on the corridor and home to Central Washington University. Past Kittitas, you'll find another detour for an impassable bridge over I-90. The trail leaves the irrigated agricultural land and enters the bleak, dry landscape of the Yakima Training Center, where the trail then drops into the basin carved by the Pacific Northwest's largest river, the Columbia. The 2,200-foot-long Beverly Bridge across the river is closed, however, and travelers need to detour upriver to the crossing at Vantage.

Trail users return to irrigated farmland and wildlife refuges east of the Columbia River, beginning in Beverly. Travelers will encounter many interruptions in the corridor between here and the Idaho border, due to private ownership, missing trestles, rockslides, and year-round flooding. The longest detours are between Smyrna and Warden, Ralston and Marengo, and Ewan and Kenova.

The DNR requires travelers east of the Columbia River to obtain a permit, which includes the combination for locked gates and a map showing detours. (Contact the DNR Southeast Region: 509-925-8510.)

Visitors are urged to carry plenty of water and food because the towns are few and far between.

CONTACT: **parks.wa.gov/DocumentCenter/Home/View/885** or **mtsgreenway.org**

DIRECTIONS

To reach the Cedar Falls trailhead, take I-90 to Exit 32. Head south on 436th Ave. SE/Cedar Falls Road for 4 miles. Pass the Rattlesnake Lake Recreation Area entrance, and turn left into Iron Horse State Park.

To reach the trailhead at Tekoa, head south on US 195 from Spokane for 32 miles. Take the WA 271 S exit, and go 8.5 miles, and then turn left onto WA 27 N/Tekoa Oaksdale Road. In 11.2 miles, the road becomes Ramsey St. in Tekoa. In 0.3 mile, bear left at a T-intersection, and turn right onto Washington St. The trail is two blocks past Poplar St.

A Discover Pass, displayed in your motor vehicle, is required at trailheads.

Discover a rare trail adventure in the hills above the Columbia River as you traverse a remote canyon and a National Scenic Area, as well as 11 miles of nationally designated Wild and Scenic River, along the Klickitat Trail.

The 1903 Columbia River & Northern Railroad line paralleled the Klickitat River for much of its 42 miles from Goldendale to Lyle, transporting food goods, livestock, and lumber to steamships on the Columbia. In 1908, the Spokane, Portland & Seattle Railway lined the Washington shore and absorbed the short line. Lyle became a vital shipping point for sheep and wheat, while passengers rode the line to Portland. The BNSF Railway operated the line from 1970 to the early 1990s, when the Klickitat lumber mill closed.

Now, almost 30 miles of scenic trail climb from the Columbia River to the Goldendale Plateau. A missing trestle divides the trail into two parts at the northern tip;

The Wild and Scenic Klickitat River, which feeds into the Columbia River, is a main feature of this trail.

County
Klickitat

Endpoints
Lewis and Clark Hwy./
WA 14 at WA 142 (Lyle)
to Centerville Hwy. at
Uecker Road (Centerville)

Mileage
29.6

Roughness Index
2

Surface
Dirt, Gravel

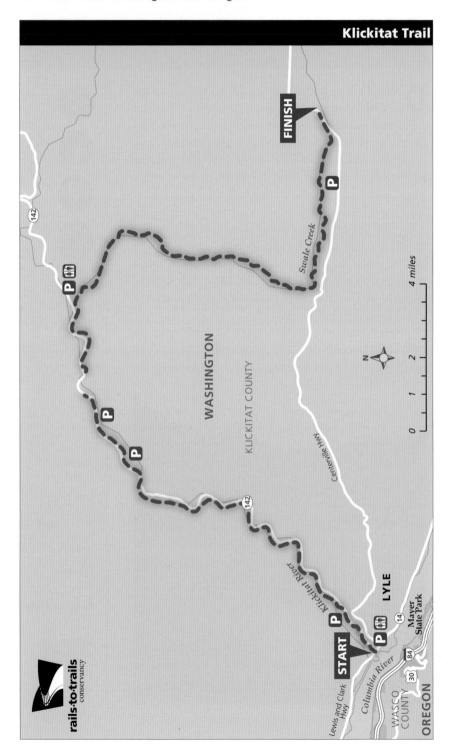

therefore, you must experience each part separately. Here, the trail also experiences a transition zone, creating two distinct landscapes with separate climates.

Crushed gravel lines the western 13.2 miles of trail from Lyle to Klickitat. (Note: This is the only portion of the trail open to equestrians.) After traveling 1.7 miles, you'll reach the boundary of the Columbia River National Scenic Area and cross the Fisher Hill Trestle to the west bank, away from the highway. Oaks and ponderosa pines abound along the Klickitat riverside, where eagles congregate in winter and wildflowers bloom in spring. This trail section ends at a 3-mile detour through the town of Klickitat, around a missing trestle. From here, you can hike to a beach and a dry ice plant created in the 1930s (and supported by the area's once-prevalent mineral springs).

The contrasting beauty of the remote Swale Canyon begins east of Klickitat and continues southeast for 16.4 miles, passing below basalt cliffs (on a somewhat rocky, irregular surface) to the open prairie flatlands of the Golden Plateau. Due to its dryness and potential fire dangers, this section of trail is only open from October through June.

Note: Brief gaps and technical areas require dismounts for bikers. The only way in or out of the canyon is at the trailheads, and solo travel is discouraged. To enjoy this extraordinary backcountry safely, go to **klickitat-trail.org** to access precautions, guidelines, and essential tips for hikers and mountain bikers.

CONTACT: klickitat-trail.org

DIRECTIONS

To reach the Lyle trailhead from the Portland area, take I-84 to Exit 64, and cross the Hood River Bridge to Washington. Turn right (east) onto WA 14, and travel 13 miles. Cross the Klickitat River Bridge at the entrance to Lyle, and turn left (north) onto WA 142. Turn left at the trailhead entrance in 100 yards.

To reach the Harms Road trailhead from Lyle, head northeast for 15 miles on the paved Lyle-Centerville Hwy. Turn left (north) onto Harms Road. Go 0.5 mile, and park just north of the bridge.

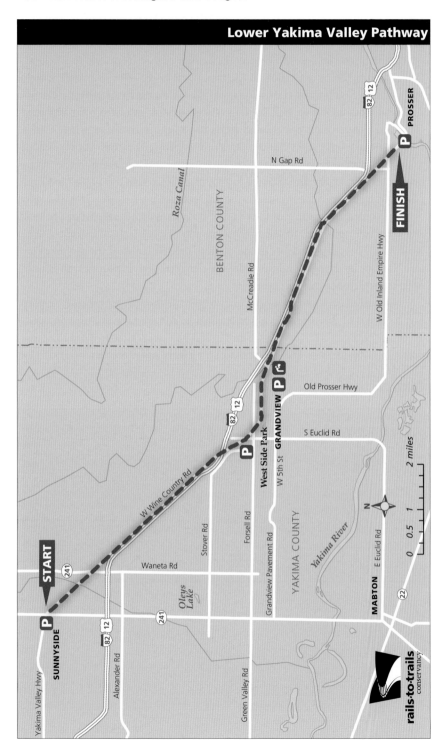

Lower Yakima Valley Pathway

The Lower Yakima Valley Pathway offers trail users the opportunity to experience great wines (produced from grapes grown in the area's rich volcanic-ash soil), interesting shops, and local hospitality and entertainment as they traverse three desert towns along the 14-mile paved route.

Once part of the North Coast Railroad and the Oregon-Washington Railroad & Navigation Company, the trail parallels the Yakima Valley Highway, I-82, and Wine Country Road, beginning on the eastern edge of Sunnyside (by the Mid Valley Mall) and ending in Prosser. The route takes you 6.5 miles to Grandview (you'll pass by the town's commercial districts on US 12/Wine Country Road). Be prepared for a variety of conditions, including extremely hot summers—the path offers little shade—and colder fall temperatures.

The 8-foot-wide trail sports some hills and road crossings, and cyclists and skaters are encouraged to use

The perfect pairing: a stroll along the Lower Yakima Valley Pathway followed by a tasting at a local winery

Counties
Benton, Yakima

Endpoints
Yakima Valley Hwy. at Mid Valley Mall (Sunnyside) to Wine Country Road at Yakima River (Prosser)

Mileage
14

Roughness Index
1

Surface
Asphalt

caution and be aware of pedestrians. You will reach a 1.5-mile section on the roadway from Grandview Park & Ride to the East Grandview trailhead, where water is available. The gap ends at the Palacios Parkway archway on the north side of the road at mile 8.

The next 6 miles to Prosser make for a rural experience; note that fewer services are available along this part of the route. At mile 11.5, you'll find an active trestle crossing; avoid this by dipping down from the right-of-way. The trail officially ends immediately before a bridge and pathway that crosses the Yakima River and takes you into downtown Prosser.

CONTACT: ci.sunnyside.wa.us/Facilities/Facility/Details/Lower-Valley-Pathway-14

DIRECTIONS

Take I-82 to Exit 69 for Sunnyside. Head north on WA 241/Waneta Road for 0.4 mile. Turn left onto Yakima Valley Hwy. In 1.2 miles, parking is available by the Mid Valley Mall (Yakima Valley Hwy. and E. Edison Ave.).

Grandview Park & Ride and the East Grandview trailhead are on CR 12/Wine Country Road. Take I-82 to Exit 75. Turn right onto Mcreadie Road, and immediately turn right onto CR 12/Wine Country Road. In 0.4 mile, look for the trail on the right.

To reach the trailhead in Prosser, take I-82 to Exit 82. Head west on Wine Country Road for 1.7 miles. Street parking is available at the Yakima River in Prosser.

20 Olympic Discovery Trail: Blyn to Elwha River

The 37 miles of Olympic Discovery Trail sandwiched between Sequim Bay and the Elwha River are considered the trail system's crown jewel. Bounded by a sparkling tidal estuary in the east and a recently undammed river in the west, the rail-trail visits the towns of Sequim and Port Angeles as it crosses the base of the Olympic Mountains. The route is divided into three segments here: Blyn to Sequim, Sequim to Port Angeles, and Port Angeles to the Elwha River.

The route follows the corridor of the Seattle, Port Angeles & Western Railway, constructed between Port Angeles and Discovery Bay from 1914 to 1915. The railway linked with the Port Townsend & Southern Railroad but didn't connect to a main line. The railroad solved the problem by using barges to transport railroad cars across Puget Sound. The railway had the distinction of being the only one in the nation whose schedule was determined

County
Clallam

Endpoints
Jamestown S'Klallam Reservation at Old Blyn Hwy. (Blyn) to Elwha River Road at the Elwha River (Port Angeles)

Mileage
37.1

Roughness Index
1

Surface
Asphalt

There are many opportunities for quiet reflection along this beautiful stretch of the Olympic Discovery Trail from Blyn to the Elwha River.

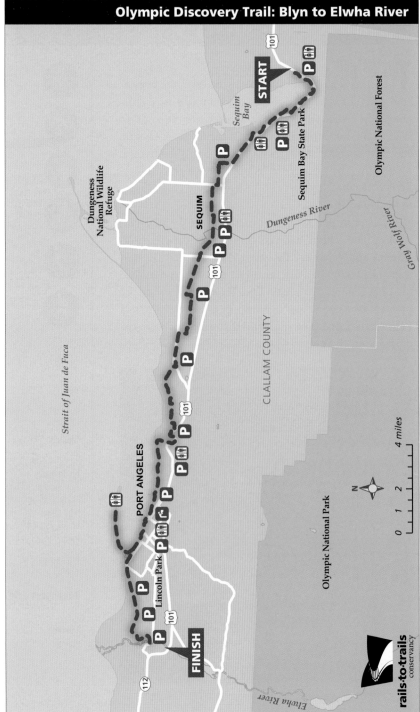

by the tides. By 1931, the railroad had discontinued passenger service, and the Chicago, Milwaukee, St. Paul and Pacific Railroad had acquired the line to haul freight and timber. The Seattle & North Coast Railroad bought the railway in 1981 and reinstituted passenger service between Port Angeles and Port Townsend. It didn't take hold, however, and crews began removing track in 1985. Soon after, the Peninsula Trails Coalition formed to build a trail.

Blyn to Sequim: 7.5 miles

This piece of the Olympic Discovery Trail starts at the Jamestown S'Klallam Reservation in Blyn and skirts Sequim Bay through a forested state park, ending in the town of Sequim (pronounced "skwim").

The rail-trail actually starts in the woods, about 0.6 mile east of the tribal headquarters, but there's no parking. Plans call for extending the trail 2.5 miles east to a new trailhead and parking lot. The tribe's small reservation includes the facilities you can see from the Blyn trailhead at the library, as well as the 7 Cedars Casino across US 101. As you follow the trail west and join Old Blyn Highway, it's not uncommon to see people digging for clams in Sequim Bay at low tide. The trail reappears on the left in 0.25 mile, crosses a couple of bridges over Jimmycomelately Creek, and begins climbing in the woods bordering the bay.

The path joins Dawley Road and crosses the Schoolhouse Point Lane intersection at mile 2.1. Just beyond, the trail turns right into the Camp Ramblewood Environmental Learning Center. You'll need to watch for the small, blue Olympic Discovery Trail markings as you descend the winding road through Sequim Bay State Park past towering firs and cedars. Hiker-biker campsites are available here for trail users. The path climbs out of the park and crosses Discovery Creek on a 150-foot-long restored trestle within earshot of US 101. The trail arrives at Whitefeather Way trailhead at mile 4.8 and crosses Johnson Creek trestle. At 410 feet long and 86 feet above the creek, it's the largest on the peninsula. Built in 1914, it was curved and banked for stability. Volunteers converted the trestle for trail use, even repurposing the water storage platforms with benches.

The route leaves the forest and rolls across an arid prairie toward Sequim. The high peaks of the Olympic Mountains to the south create a rain shadow over the region that's responsible for sunny, dry weather. Meteorological data shows that Sequim gets only 16 inches of rain annually, compared to 26 inches for Port Angeles. The west end of this trail section on the Elwha River gets more than 40 inches, and the eastern end of Crescent Lake gets 70 inches. No wonder Sequim is a popular retirement community.

Following the path along East Washington Street, the route turns right at Rhodefer Road at 6.4 miles, across from the visitor center, and continues into Carrie Blake Park. The trail goes around the park perimeter to restrooms and parking at Blake Avenue and Fir Street.

Carrie Blake Park in Sequim to Port Angeles City Pier: 20.1 miles

A couple of creek crossings account for the steepest terrain on this mostly level trail section that stretches from the retirement community in Sequim to the bustling waterfront in Port Angeles.

Leaving Carrie Blake Park, the Olympic Discovery Trail heads due west on Fir Street, north (right) on North Sequim Avenue, and west (left) on the paved trail on the north side of West Hendrickson Road. Traveling through Sequim neighborhoods, the trail turns left onto a path next to North Priest Road at 2.3 miles and finds the railroad grade on the right at 2.5 miles. Just ahead is Railroad Bridge Park, where the Dungeness River rages past. Exhibits at the Dungeness River Audubon Center here include displays of local wildlife and a native plant garden. The restored railroad trestle—the first acquisition for the Olympic Discovery Trail—is one of the few remaining wood truss railroad bridges, completely made from timbers, except for its steel tension bars. A 610-foot trestle extension on the west side crosses the floodplain. Note: A portion of this trail (encompassing the railroad bridge) has been closed due to trestle damage caused by a February 2015 flood. Until repairs are made, people using the trail must take a detour around the closed section; a recommended route to the south has been posted. An equestrian side path starts at the trailhead on the west end of the bridge. The railroad grade continues across farmland and prairie and passes the Sequim Valley Airport. The trail crosses Kitchen-Dick Road at mile 6. (For a side trip, consider heading north 3 miles to the Dungeness National Wildlife Refuge on the Strait of Juan de Fuca. You can hike 5.5 miles to a lighthouse on the Dungeness Spit, one of the longest natural sandspits in the world. Clallam County operates a campground nearby.) In 0.5 mile, the trail turns south along the side of Vautier Road and then enters Robin Hill Farm County Park.

More than 3 miles of hiking trails and 2.5 miles of equestrian trails wind through the forest, meadows, and wetlands in the park. The National Park Service grows native plants here for the revegetation of the Elwha River valley, where a dam was removed to restore a free-flowing river.

The trail crosses McDonald Creek on a 93-foot-long railroad flatcar bed converted into a bridge. Following Barr and Abbott Roads, the trail runs through pastureland before joining a path on Spring Road. The route continues west along Old Olympic Highway and ducks under the highway at mile 10.7 to cross a creek. Leaving the farmland behind, the path surroundings transform to second-growth forest over the next 3 miles.

At mile 14, the trail enters a forested ravine and descends to the Bagley Creek covered bridge, formerly a Bainbridge Island ferry ramp. You'll want to give way to cyclists descending from the west, who may encounter a dangerous combination of a slippery surface and the sharp turn to the bridge. Ascending to US 101, a good vista of the Olympic Mountains can be enjoyed at the Deer Park

Overlook. The trail passes the Morse Creek trailhead, reenters the woods, and makes a steep, 150-foot plunge to the Morse Creek trestle.

The trail heads north past a residential neighborhood for a mile and abruptly arrives at the Strait of Juan de Fuca with spectacular views along the coast and across the water to Canada. The 4-mile path to downtown Port Angeles hugs the shoreline, allowing opportunities to spot birds and sea life. The Ediz Hook sandspit that protects the Port Angeles harbor can be seen after turning onto the waterfront trail, soon followed by views of historic buildings in downtown.

Arriving at City Pier, you will discover opportunities for shopping, dining, and lodging. The Feiro Marine Life Center features a touch tank for aquatic life, and a tower provides views of the mountains and strait. A ferry offers service to Victoria, and buses at the transit center can give travelers a lift back to Sequim.

Port Angeles City Pier to Elwha River: 7.1 miles

Leaving behind the busy maritime district in Port Angeles, this route climbs to views overlooking the Strait of Juan de Fuca and ends at the Elwha River, site of the biggest dam removal project in history.

The Olympic Discovery Trail is also known as the Port Angeles Waterfront Trail as it heads west along the north side of Railroad Avenue, Front Street, and Marine Drive. Passing several shops, cafés, and marine businesses, it forks to the right 1.8 miles from City Pier to sail out toward the Coast Guard station on Ediz Hook. The sandspit extends to picnic areas, parks, and beaches, where visitors can scan the horizon for orca pods, identify birds, or look for marine life. Sail & Paddle Park features a special area for people with disabilities.

Instead of heading right to Ediz Hook, however, this route takes the left fork, crossing Marine Drive and climbing the aptly named West Hill Street. (Though both sides of the street have shoulders, the south side is wider to accommodate trail traffic.) Stenciled emblems on the road direct travelers onto West Fourth Street, where Crown Park presents views over the harbor. The route turns right onto South Milwaukee Drive, which leads to the West 10th Street trailhead at 3.1 miles. The path resumes on the peaceful, wooded railroad corridor. The West 18th Street trailhead is just down the trail at 3.8 miles, and the trail passes the end of an airport runway before it crosses Dry Creek and arrives at the Kacee Way trailhead (4.9 miles), donated by the Lower Elwha Klallam tribe. Deer and smaller wildlife are frequently seen roaming the area surrounding the path.

The trail descends gradually for 1.5 miles into the lush Elwha River floodplain. A trail bridge suspended beneath the 589-foot-long Elwha River Bridge, completed in 2009, enables unobstructed views up and down the river. From here, or down below at river level, visitors can see islands of sediment slowly migrating downstream. The sand was released from behind 100-year-old dams that the federal government began removing in 2012. As a result, salmon are returning to spawn upriver.

Though the trail ends here, a temporary on-road route continues west toward Joyce and Lake Crescent. Consult **olympicdiscoverytrail.com** for details.

CONTACT: olympicdiscoverytrail.com

DIRECTIONS

To reach Blyn, from the intersection of WA 20 and US 101 near Port Townsend, take US 101 W for 11.3 miles. Turn right onto Blyn Crossing (opposite Snow Creek Road), and then turn right again at the T-intersection onto Old Blyn Hwy. Pass by the Jamestown S'Klallam Tribal Headquarters. In 0.4 mile, park at the library on the right at the end of the complex.

To reach Carrie Blake Park in Sequim, from the intersection of WA 20 and US 101 near Port Townsend, take US 101 W for 15.9 miles. Exit onto E. Washington St. After traveling approximately 0.9 mile, turn right onto S. Blake Ave. In 0.3 mile, access the trail, parking, and restrooms at E. Fir St. and N. Blake Ave. Clallam County Transit buses carry bike racks. Schedule and routes are available at **clallamtransit.com/routes-by-number.html.**

For trail access at Port Angeles City Pier, from Sequim, take US 101 W about 16 miles. Turn right onto N. Lincoln St. in Port Angeles. Turn right for parking at City Pier.

For Elwha River bridge parking, take US 101 W from Port Angeles about 4.5 miles. Turn right onto Laird Road. In 0.7 mile, turn left onto Elwha River Road. In another 0.7 mile, turn left onto Crown Z Water Road, which leads to a water treatment plant beneath the bridge.

21 Olympic Discovery Trail East: Port Townsend

The Port Townsend waterfront marks the eastern endpoint of the Olympic Discovery Trail, which will one day stretch 126 miles from Puget Sound to the Pacific Ocean. This section of trail is named in memory of Larry Scott, one of the many dedicated volunteers who have helped develop Olympic Peninsula trails over the past 25 years.

In 1887, Port Townsend residents formed the Port Townsend & Southern Railroad to Quilcene, and passenger and freight service began in 1890. Passenger rail service between Port Townsend and Port Angeles did not come until the early 1900s, after logging work was well under way. The regional movement to create the Olympic Discovery Trail began after railroad service was discontinued in the 1980s.

The waterfront trailhead offers a view of the marina and beyond. The intermittent, separated horse trail begins

A beautiful waterfront view awaits on this section of the Olympic Discovery Trail.

County
Jefferson

Endpoints
Boat St. and Washington St. (Port Townsend) to S. Discovery Road and Milo Curry Road (Adelma Beach)

Mileage
7.3

Roughness Index
1

Surface
Crushed Stone

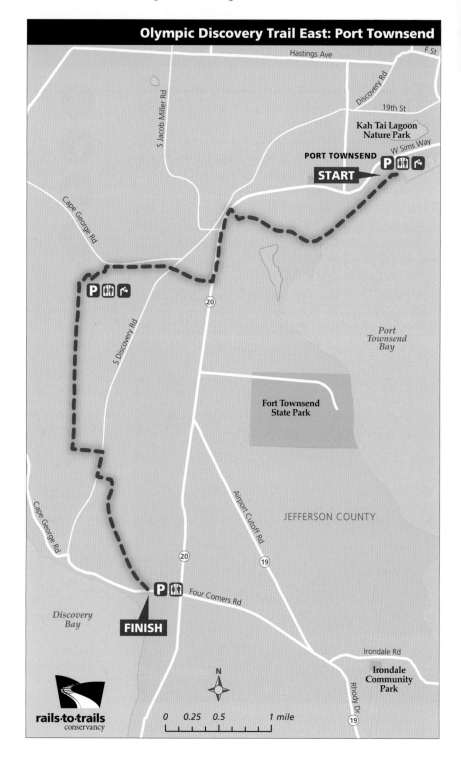

just beyond the trailhead, along with map and history kiosks. A little climb to two road crossings introduces you to this peaceful community trail among maples, alders, firs, and ferns.

The path ascends some small inclines here and there and briefly parallels WA 20. Pass under the road at mile 2.6, as the railroad once did, and bear left. As you head up toward the road, a sign directs you to go straight to the roadside shoulder and then right to the trail. (Signs are placed on the road, inviting road riders and pedestrians to pass under WA 20 rather than cross the bridge.)

At 3 miles, you'll pass under Discovery Road and relax into rural countryside, crossing small roads every now and then. Here, an equestrian trail reappears and heads up the side of the hill. This pretty wooded section, separated from Cape George Road, meets the Cape George trailhead at 3.6 miles.

Signs direct you to cross the rural Edwards Road. You'll pass horses and a golf course hidden by trees before crossing South Discovery Road at 6.1 miles. Use caution. On the other side, you'll notice benches strategically placed atop the short hill just where the grade approaches 10%. Wind through the trees, again on the original railroad grade, and up to the Milo Curry trailhead at mile 7.3.

In addition to enjoying the trail, you may want to spend some time in Port Townsend, home of good food, great views, Victorian homes, artist shops, film festivals, and loads of natural beachfront at Fort Worden State Park.

CONTACT: olympicdiscoverytrail.com

DIRECTIONS

To reach the waterfront trailhead from the intersection of WA 20 and US 101 near Port Townsend, take WA 20 E for 7.7 miles to Port Townsend. Turn left to stay on WA 20. Go 3.8 miles (WA 20 will become W. Sims Way). Turn right at the Haines Pl. traffic light, and go straight into the boatyard, toward the water. Park near the restroom.

To reach the Milo Curry trailhead from the intersection of WA 20 and US 101 near Port Townsend, take WA 20 E for 6.2 miles. Turn left onto S. Discovery Road. In 0.3 mile, turn right onto Milo Curry Road. Fork left to the trailhead.

Horse trailer turnarounds and portable toilets are available at Milo Curry and Cape George.

Olympic Discovery Trail: Spruce Railroad Trail

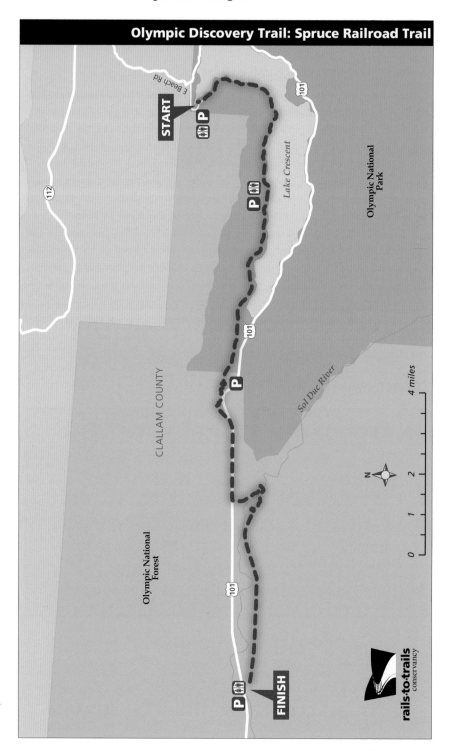

22 Olympic Discovery Trail: Spruce Railroad Trail

Sitka spruce is unique to the temperate rain forests of the coastal Pacific Northwest. Its strong, light wood was found to be particularly useful for World War I–era airplanes, so the U.S. Army built the Spruce Railroad to transport this strategic lumber from the coastal forests to Port Angeles. World War I ended just 19 days after completion of the railroad, however, so commercial logging companies took over the 36-mile rail line and used it until 1954.

To remember the rail line, the section of the Olympic Discovery Trail that runs through the Olympic National Forest has been named the Spruce Railroad Trail. Plans call for paving the often narrow, winding, rocky dirt trail. When improvements are complete, the entire 19.6-mile stretch of the Olympic Discovery Trail from the East Beach Road trailhead to the Camp Creek trailhead will be a paved corridor (with 2 miles on US 101).

Lakes tucked within the temperate rain forests of the peninsula are hidden gems along the Olympic Discovery Trail.

County
Clallam

Endpoints
E. Beach Road at Lake Crescent (Port Angeles) to Cooper Ranch Road at US 101 (Beaver)

Mileage
19.6

Roughness Index
2–3

Surface
Asphalt, Dirt

East Beach Road (Lyre River) Trailhead to Sol Duc Road Parking Lot:
10.1 miles

Visitors to this remote section of trail will likely be awed by the beauty of Lake Crescent and the grand views of forested mountains across the crystal-clear blue water. The segment rolls along the north shore of the glacier-formed lake within the boundaries of Olympic National Park.

In 1938, President Franklin Roosevelt established the 922,650 acres of rain forest, extensive old-growth forest, glacier-topped peaks, and alpine meadows as Olympic National Park. Its forests are home to cougars, bears, deer, woodpeckers, golden eagles, mountain goats, and peregrine falcons nesting above the trail on Pyramid Mountain. Lake Crescent contains several unique species of fish.

Starting at the East Beach Road (Lyre River) trailhead, the 8-foot-wide paved trail quickly reverts to snaky 2- to 4-foot-wide dirt singletrack. It is rocky and rough in some places and flat in others—easy for hikers and a bit beyond moderate for average mountain bikers. Stretches of trail skirt the edge of an occasionally undercut shoreline, but elsewhere the path climbs 200 feet above the lake. Long pants and bright colors are recommended to protect trail users from deer ticks. Also keep an eye out for the "leaves of three," or poison oak.

Work is scheduled to continue every summer through 2017 or 2018 to upgrade and pave this nearly 4-mile dirt segment of the Spruce Railroad Trail to universal accessibility standards. Visitors should expect trail closures during work season.

The trail rises gently into a forest of giant cedars, Douglas firs, red alders, and Pacific madrones amid a dense understory of salal. The path then makes one of its frequent visits to the shoreline, dropping to clearings where the Olympic Mountains can be seen across the lake.

Trail users can visit two railroad tunnels at miles 1.1 and 3.0 from the trailhead. The entrances have been partially blasted shut, so the route detours around them at the edge of the lake. The first detour crosses a bridge around a swimming hole called Devil's Punchbowl, a small, deep cove of turquoise waters and steep rock walls that form the base of Pyramid Mountain. The upgrade plans include reopening the tunnels for trail use.

After the second tunnel, the route follows the bumpy railroad grade uphill, hitting paved trail at about 4.1 miles from the East Beach Road (Lyre River) trailhead. (A path that forks to the left here goes to the Camp David Junior Road trailhead and parking lot. This lightly used road connects to Fairholm on US 101.)

The paved trail follows the contour of the mountain to the former station site of Ovington, now nothing more than a signpost. A short path to the left heads to restrooms, parking, and picnic tables at North Shore trailhead. Camp David Junior Road also passes here for a 3.3-mile return to US 101 at Fairholm. To the right is a hiking trail leading to the top of Pyramid Mountain.

The wide asphalt path follows the railroad grade uphill toward Fairholm Summit over the next 4.5 miles. Views of the lake are nearly obscured by the dense forest.

As you leave Olympic National Park in this area, the trail name changes to Olympic Discovery Trail. Just before the top of the climb, a 0.2-mile paved trail forks downhill to the left toward the Sol Duc Road parking lot on US 101. (A right turn continues almost 10 miles west toward the Camp Creek trailhead.)

Sol Duc Road Parking Lot to Camp Creek Trailhead: 9.5 miles

The Olympic Discovery Trail keeps pushing westward toward the rain forests, where the hemlock, spruce, cedar, and fir trees grow larger, and the ferns and moss grow denser. The route briefly follows US 101 and a U.S. Forest Service road before it picks up on an old railbed that parallels the serpentine Sol Duc River. The 1951 Great Forks Fire sparked in this area, roaring across 18 miles of dry summer landscape to burn more than 30,000 acres of forest and more than 30 buildings in Forks.

The route starts at the Sol Duc Road parking lot, following a 0.2-mile access trail to the paved Olympic Discovery Trail. Turning left at the junction, the trail climbs a series of tight switchbacks that are noticeably steeper than a railroad grade and arrives at Fairholm summit in 0.4 mile. The trail crosses a couple of bridges and passes a connection to the Mount Muller Trail on the way downhill to US 101 in less than a mile.

For the next 2.1 miles, the route takes the shoulder of US 101, where a steady procession of logging trucks serves as a reminder that this is timber country. The first road on the left is Forest Service Road 2918, where you'll carefully cross US 101. (Future plans call for a paved trail running south of the highway.)

Following FS 2918, the trail enters a working forest. Unlike the protected forests in Olympic National Park, the woods here have been logged at least once. Trees in some tracts have a striking uniformity. Travelers on foot, bike, or horse may encounter logging trucks at any time. Warning signs suggest getting off the road at the first hint of a truck.

After about a mile, the path turns right onto another Forest Service road that crosses Sol Duc River, whose name translates to "sparkling waters." The road climbs after the bridge and picks up the old railroad grade on the right. This last leg of wide, paved rail-trail heads gradually downhill over the next 5 miles, passing through stately forests and recently logged areas to the Camp Creek trailhead.

The Olympic Discovery Trail continues west on 30 miles of roads and highways described at the website. The westward route ends at 1.5 miles of separated trail that connect to the Pacific Ocean beaches at La Push.

CONTACT: olympicdiscoverytrail.com

DIRECTIONS

To reach the E. Beach Road (Lyre River) trailhead, head west from Port Angeles on US 101, and go approximately 15 miles. Turn right onto paved E. Beach Road, following signs for LOG CABIN RESORT. After 3.1 miles, pass the resort and follow a sign to the left marked SPRUCE RAILROAD TRAIL. Reach the trailhead in 0.8 mile.

To reach the Sol Duc Road parking lot, take US 101 W from Port Angeles for approximately 28 miles. After passing Lake Crescent, look for an Olympic National Park sign that reads SOL DUC VALLEY HOT SPRINGS RESORT. Turn right into a roadside parking lot across from Sol Duc Road.

To reach the Camp Creek trailhead, from Port Angeles, take US 101 W for 35 miles. Turn left at mile marker 211 onto Cooper Ranch Road (Klahowya Campground is on the right), and turn left into the trailhead. From Forks, travel northeast on US 101 for 20 miles, and turn right onto Cooper Ranch Road.

The 6.5-mile paved Preston-Snoqualmie Trail meanders through Snoqualmie Valley, with a short roadside section and crossing. It crosses a set of unpaved yet accommodating switchbacks that replace a trestle from the old Seattle, Lake Shore & Eastern Railway. This inserts a brief walk that works fine with a road bike.

The main trail leaves the Preston trailhead on a gradual, steady coast to the Raging River Valley. Preston is a historic mill town named after railway official William Preston. The area offers quiet distractions, such as an inviting grassy pullout and bench and a bridge, framed by evergreens and cedars above and the ravine below. The trail grade increases and suddenly curves sharply, steeply, and briefly toward the road at 2.5 miles. A final leveling out allows a semicivilized descent. A crosswalk and sign guide you across speedy Preston–Fall City Road

Don't let these switchbacks discourage you; the vantage points that you gain on this trail are well worth the effort.

County
King

Endpoints
300th Ave. SE and SE High Point Way (Preston) to SE David Powell Road near the Snoqualmie River (Snoqualmie)

Mileage
6.5

Roughness Index
2

Surface
Asphalt

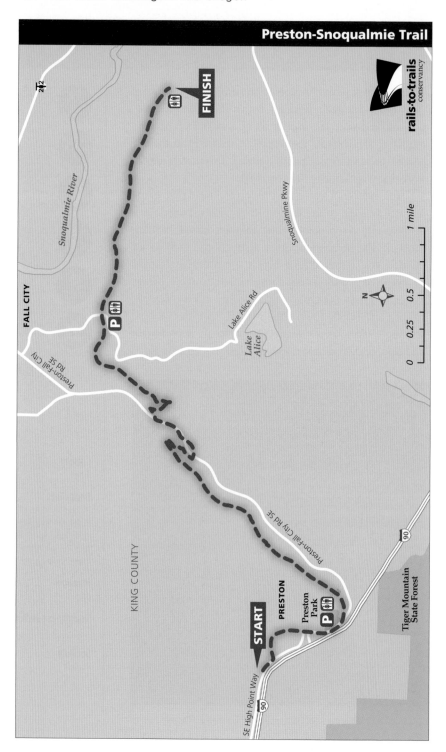

to one block of separated trail, which then takes you left onto Southeast 68th Street to a mossy bridge overlooking the river. This pleasant, short street rises to the road (with cement barriers for 0.25 mile). Abandon the road to welcome the attractive configuration of switchbacks. Climb 80 feet on grass and gravel to a well-placed bench. This older paved trail hosts a unique log chair and a bridge high above a creek. Next stop is the Lake Alice trailhead and picnic area at 3.5 miles. Parking at this trailhead offers a trip on a gentle, paved grade in either direction. From here, the trail continues 1.8 miles across Lake Alice Road. Three benches at the end of the trail provide the perfect spot to enjoy a densely framed view across Snoqualmie Falls and the river to the impressive Salish Lodge. The dense foliage of summer obstructs the view of the 270-foot waterfall, so you might want to check out this trail in fall and winter.

CONTACT: kingcounty.gov/recreation/parks/trails/regionaltrailssystem.aspx

DIRECTIONS

To reach the Preston-Snoqualmie Trailhead, take I-90 to Exit 22. At the end of the ramp, head east; then turn right at the T onto SE High Point Way. After 0.4 mile, turn left onto SE 87th Pl.

To reach the Lake Alice trailhead, continue 3.5 miles past SE 87th Pl. on SE High Point Way, which becomes Preston–Fall City Road SE. Turn right onto SE 47th St./Lake Alice Road SE; the parking lot will be 0.8 mile uphill on the right. The final 1.8-mile section begins across the road.

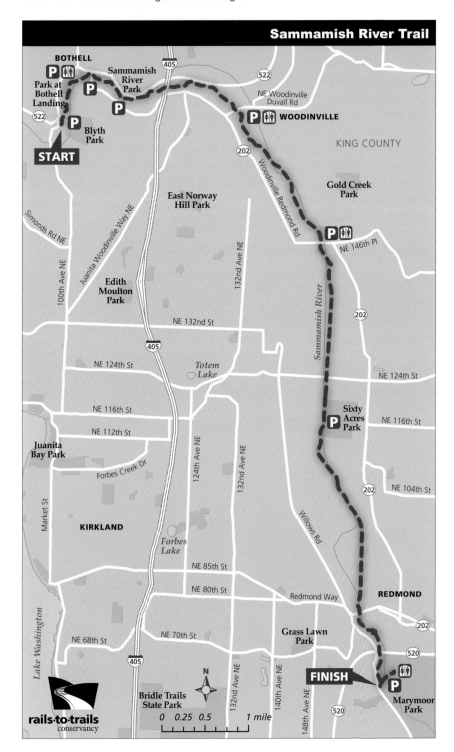

24 Sammamish River Trail

The Sammamish River Trail rolls along smoothly through a wide, scenic greenway that's home to riverside parks and farms, as well as a growing wine industry. The trail is the center link of the Seattle area's locks-to-lakes corridor, which connects the Ballard Locks to Lakes Washington and Sammamish via the Burke-Gilman and East Lake Sammamish rail-trails.

Yet the Sammamish River Trail isn't a rail-trail. It's a levee trail that was created in the 1960s when crews drained the swamps and completed the second rechanneling of the one-time meandering Sammamish River. The wide asphalt trail follows the river for 11 miles, from Bothell's Blyth Park in the north (where it connects to the Burke-Gilman Trail; see page 11) to Redmond's Marymoor Park in the south (where it links to the Marymoor Connector and East Lake Sammamish Trail; see page 34).

A variety of wildlife shares this river corridor; look for weasels, beavers, herons, and more.

County
King

Endpoints
Blyth Park (Bothell)
to Marymoor Park
(Redmond)

Mileage
11

Roughness Index
1

Surface
Asphalt

Passing through the population centers of Bothell, Woodinville, and Redmond, the trail is one of King County's busiest. Visitors are drawn here by the open spaces; the views of far-off Mount Rainier and the closer Cascade foothills; and the opportunity to hike, run, skate, or ride a bike or a horse (a soft-surface side trail for equestrians is accessible between Northeast 175th Street in Woodinville to Marymoor Park). Bike commuters roll through here in the mornings and evenings, and lunchtime strollers fill the Redmond section on sunny weekdays.

To start at Blyth Park in Bothell, leave the parking lot and turn left. Turn right onto a trail heading north, and then turn left at a sign pointing to the Sammamish River Trail and bear right at the next junction. The river supports lush surroundings here. A bridge crosses the river for a possible side trip to historical buildings at Bothell Landing. The trail meanders east and then trends southward at Woodinville's Wilmot Gateway Park, which sports a grape arbor. Maples and alders grow along the river, while picnic tables, benches, and soccer and baseball fields inhabit the grassy areas by the trail. Weasels, hooded mergansers, painted turtles, beavers, frogs, salmon, and herons share the river, and hawks and bald eagles patrol the sky.

Farther south, an off-route trail option follows Northeast 145th Street westward to the Hollywood Winery District, where both notable and little-known wines are poured in tasting rooms. A brewery and restaurant can be found there as well.

The route passes agricultural land and athletic fields on its approach to Redmond—where the path can get crowded on weekdays. It passes a government complex and senior center south of Northeast 90th Street in a trail section known as "The Stroll." At an old trestle, the river trail crosses the Redmond Central Connector, which uses an inactive BNSF railroad right-of-way to access downtown. After a couple of river crossings, the route ends at 640-acre Marymoor Park, where cyclists can take a spin in the velodrome, and all visitors can find the Marymoor Connector Trail that joins the East Lake Sammamish Trail.

CONTACT: kingcounty.gov/recreation/parks/trails/regionaltrailssystem.aspx

DIRECTIONS

To reach Blyth Park from I-405, take Exit 23 to WA 522 west toward Seattle. After 0.2 mile, bear right onto Kaysner Way. Turn left onto Main St. After 0.1 mile, turn left onto 102nd Ave. NE. When the road ends at 0.3 mile, turn right onto W. Riverside Dr. Blyth Park is 0.5 mile ahead.

To reach Marymoor Park from I-405, take Exit 14. Follow WA 520 E for 4.7 miles, and exit to W. Lake Sammamish Pkwy. NE. Turn right, and go 0.2 mile. Turn left into Marymoor Park at the signal at NE Marymoor Way. The trail begins at the first lot on the left by the tennis courts.

25 Similkameen Trail

The Similkameen Trail follows a river by the same name that drains the high country across the border in British Columbia. The dirt and gravel rail-trail crosses a scenic high bridge to enter a dramatic river gorge that leads to a waterfall. But at 3.5 miles, the trail ends short of the Canadian border.

Built in 1907 by the Washington & Great Northern Railroad (which would merge with other rail lines to become the Burlington Northern Railroad in 1970), the original tracks fell into disuse in 1972 when a record flood caused bridge damage on the line. As one of the most biologically diverse watersheds in western North America, the cross-border valley is home to grizzly bears, wolves, lynx, fishers, wolverines, elk, snowshoe hares, mule deer, owls, woodpeckers, and a great diversity of birds, including eagles and falcons.

County
Okanogan

Endpoints
Kernan Road to Enloe Dam on the Similkameen River (Oroville)

Mileage
3.5

Roughness Index
2

Surface
Dirt, Gravel

The Similkameen Trail explores one of the most biologically diverse watersheds in North America.

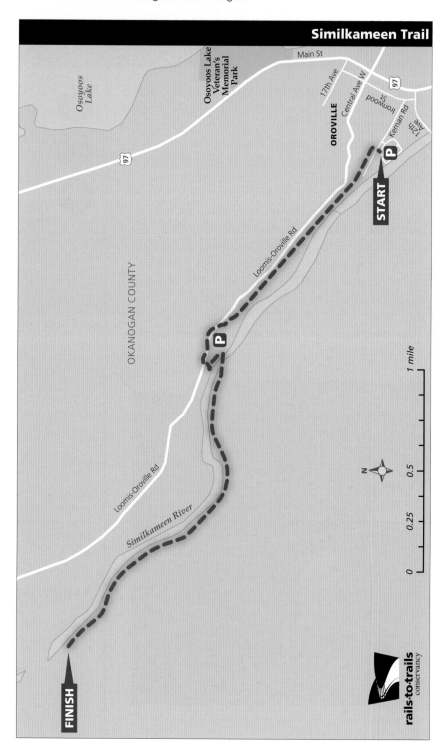

Beginning on the west side of Oroville, the path has an easy grade, despite the nearby Okanogan Highlands and Cascade Range. High temperatures here can soar to 100°F in the summer or drop to 30°F in the winter. Snow cover is possible between November and March.

In a setting of shrub steppe and occasional evergreens, the trail passes Taber's trailhead about 1.5 miles from the Oroville trailhead and crosses the Similkameen River gorge on a 375-foot-long girder bridge. In season, salmon and steelhead runs can be seen 90 feet below in the river.

Passing benches, interpretive displays, and views of the river, the route currently ends at a gate with a vista of the nearly 100-year-old Enloe Dam and the waterfalls variously known as Coyote, Similkameen, or Enloe Falls. Okanogan County plans to push through the gate and extend the trail along the former rail corridor, including a 0.6-mile tunnel, to the mining ghost town of Nighthawk. The expansion will bring the trail closer to the Canadian border and the popular Kettle Valley Rail Trail network there.

The Old Oroville Depot Museum and Visitor Center, near the Oroville trailhead at 1210 Ironwood Street, has permanent and temporary displays of history and culture.

CONTACT: okanogancountry.com/locations/maps/urban-walking-trails

DIRECTIONS

To reach the Oroville trailhead from the intersection of WA 20 and US 97 in Okanogan, follow US 97 N for approximately 45 miles to Oroville. Turn left onto 12th Ave., and then go one block to the Old Oroville Depot Museum at the corner of 12th Ave. and Ironwood St. The trailhead is just up the street from the museum; follow signs.

To reach Taber's trailhead from US 97 in Oroville, turn left onto Central Ave. W. Drive 1.7 miles on Central Ave. W, which becomes Loomis-Oroville Road, to trailhead parking on the right.

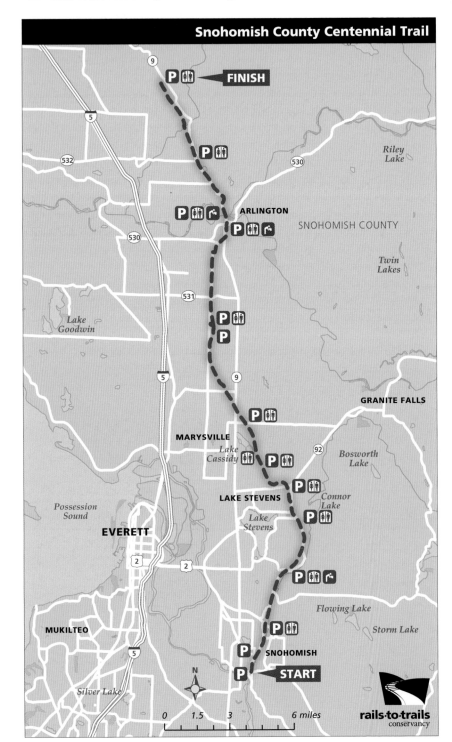

Snohomish County Centennial Trail

26 Snohomish County Centennial Trail

History lures visitors to the Snohomish County Centennial Trail. Trail users are reminded of old-time river and railroad settlements in the historically preserved storefronts and homes in Snohomish and Arlington. Illustrated displays at the regularly spaced trailheads explain the social and commercial heritage of the area.

The paved trail follows the original route of the Seattle, Lake Shore & Eastern Railway, parts of which were later acquired by the Northern Pacific and Burlington Northern. The trail runs 30.5 miles from the town of Snohomish to the border of Skagit County. After the railroad corridor became inactive, local efforts began for a trail in 1989, the year of the state's centennial celebration. The first 6 miles opened in 1991. Long-range plans call for extending the route southward to King County's Burke-Gilman Trail (see page 11).

While there are some forested sections, the Snohomish County Centennial Trail is flanked by farms and pastures for the majority of its length.

County
Snohomish

Endpoints
First St. near Cady Park (Snohomish) to Nakashima Barn/North trailhead, west of WA 9 and just south of the Skagit County line (Arlington)

Mileage
30.5

Roughness Index
1

Surface
Asphalt

The Snohomish County Centennial Trail mostly rolls past farms and pastures and through forested watersheds. The path crosses creeks and rivers that drain the Cascade Mountains, whose snowy summits are visible in the east. Collectors might find it difficult to get started in Snohomish. More than a dozen antiques stores line First Street, where the trail currently starts. Better on-street parking is available at the traditional trailhead a few blocks north. Though the trail soon enters farmland on the edge of town, this is usually the busiest section. Horse riders are prohibited between the Snohomish and Pilchuck trailheads, as well as another congested section between Armar Road and Bryant. Travelers will notice some elevation gain after passing the replica train depot in Machias. After the former lumber mill town of Lake Stevens, the climb continues through a forested corridor to placid Lake Cassidy, where bicyclists gather at picnic tables or walk out onto the pier. Cresting the summit, the downhill run offers a couple of viewpoints across the valley floor clear west to the Olympic Mountains on the horizon.

The trail's approach to Arlington runs adjacent to busy 67th Avenue through a light industrial zone. Signs at the 204th Street intersection point toward a new trail alignment that takes users into historic downtown Arlington and another depot replica. Just north of here, a bridge spans the churning confluence of the North and South Forks of the Stillaguamish River.

A gleaming arch marks the junction of the Centennial with the Whitehorse Trail, another rail-trail, mostly ballast, leading to Darrington (as of 2015, most of this trail is closed due to damage caused by a mudslide). The Centennial Trail continues on the left branch across remote farm and forestland to the Nakashima Barn trailhead, which memorializes the successes and difficulties of a Japanese American family.

CONTACT: centennialtrail.com

DIRECTIONS

To reach the Snohomish trailhead from I-405, take Exit 23 onto WA 522 E. Follow WA 522 E for 2.4 miles, and exit onto WA 9 N toward Snohomish. Continue for 9.5 miles to the Snohomish exit. Turn right onto Second St. After approximately 1 mile, turn left onto Maple Ave. Go five or six blocks. Look for on-street parking on the right.

To reach the Nakashima Heritage Barn/North trailhead from I-5, take Exit 208 for WA 530 toward Arlington. Follow WA 530 E for 3.7 miles. Turn left onto WA 9. After 7.7 miles, the trailhead is on the left.

27 Snoqualmie Valley Trail

The Snoqualmie Valley Trail rolls from verdant dairy land in the north to a clear blue mountain lake in the south. Along the way, travelers are treated to numerous trestle crossings, historic towns, views of mountains and farmland, and a roaring waterfall.

The 31.5-mile packed gravel trail follows an extension of the Chicago, Milwaukee, St. Paul and Pacific Railroad (also known as the Milwaukee Road) that linked Everett in the north to the main line heading east-west over the Cascades. The Snoqualmie Valley Trail joins the former Milwaukee Road main line, now known as the John Wayne Pioneer Trail (which extends east to the Idaho border).

People on foot, bike, or horseback can expect extended flat sections and a couple of graded climbs. Trail users can choose their terrain by trailhead: Duvall to Carnation for a flat ride, Carnation to Snoqualmie Falls or North Bend

County
King

Endpoints
NE Woodinville-Duvall Road (Duvall) to Rattlesnake Lake at Cedar Falls Road (near Riverbend)

Mileage
31.5

Roughness Index
2

Surface
Ballast, Gravel

This path can be enjoyed in all seasons.

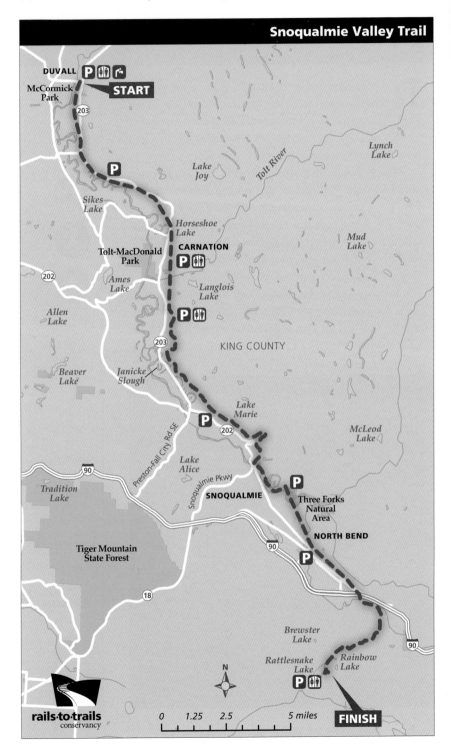

Snoqualmie Valley Trail

DUVALL

START

McCormick Park

203

Lake Joy

Tolt River

Lynch Lake

Sikes Lake

Horseshoe Lake

CARNATION

Mud Lake

Tolt-MacDonald Park

202

Ames Lake

Langlois Lake

Allen Lake

203

KING COUNTY

Beaver Lake

Janicke Slough

Lake Marie

McLeod Lake

202

90

Lake Alice

Snoqualmie Pkwy

SNOQUALMIE

Three Forks Natural Area

Tradition Lake

NORTH BEND

90

Tiger Mountain State Forest

18

Preston-Fall City Rd SE

I-90

Brewster Lake

Rattlesnake Lake

Rainbow Lake

N

rails·to·trails
conservancy

0   1.25   2.5   5 miles

FINISH

to Rattlesnake Lake for a climb, or Snoqualmie to North Bend for preserved natural features. Multiple trailheads allow easy access to smaller chunks of trail and leapfrogging with a second car.

In the north, Duvall's McCormick Park sits on the banks of the Snoqualmie River. The relocated railroad depot is restored nearby at Stephens Street and Railroad Avenue. The next 9 miles cross several farm entrances and roads en route to Carnation, which earned its name from the dairy industry that once boomed in the area and is remembered by large hay barns that dot that landscape. Wetlands, waterfowl, and songbirds create a peaceful, open setting and a barrier between trail and road. The trail arrives at Nick Loutsis Park in Carnation, where you can take a side trip a couple blocks west to visit riverside Tolt-MacDonald Park. The trail crosses the Tolt River and passes Remlinger Farms, open to the public.

Leaving Carnation, the trail begins a moderate, 400-foot climb to the upper valley. Over the next 8 miles, three trestles offer stunning valley and river views framed by evergreens. An on-road detour begins at a stairway immediately before the Tokul Road underpass at about mile 18. Climbing the stairs, the 2.5-mile detour turns right onto Tokul Road and then left onto Southeast Stearns Road. The road name changes to Mill Pond Road as it passes a lake once used by the Snoqualmie Falls Lumber Co. and Weyerhaeuser. The crumbling remnants of the mill, which at one time employed 1,200 people, are visible in the distance and remain a King County historic site. The road name changes to Southeast Reinig Road as it approaches a trestle on the right. The path resumes on the bridge deck at the top of the stairway. (To avoid the steps, turn right onto Meadowbrook Way Southeast before the trestle. Cross the Snoqualmie River on the Meadowbrook bridge, and then turn left onto Southeast Park Street. The trail is accessible on the left from a dog park path or the entrance to Mount Si Golf Course.)

A worthwhile side trip in this area joins the 1.5 million visitors a year who witness the Snoqualmie River plunging 268 feet into the valley. To visit Snoqualmie Falls, remain on Tokul Road at the detour, and turn right onto WA 202. Cross the road to Salish Lodge and the rest area overlooking the falls. From here, an alternate route back to the trail passes the extensive collection of locomotives and railcars owned by the Northwest Railway Museum in old town Snoqualmie. This option starts with a right turn onto WA 202 from the falls, crosses a bridge, and meets the Snohomish County Centennial Trail in less than a mile. The trail parallels the highway, passes the train collection, and ends at the old railroad depot, now a museum and ticket office for tourist trains. Continuing through town on WA 202/Railroad Avenue, the alternate route turns left onto Meadowbrook Way and returns to the detour.

Mount Si remains the dominant feature over the next few miles as the route crosses the trestle and passes through the Three Forks Natural Area, where the North, South, and Middle Forks of the Snoqualmie converge. A mobile fixture here is a herd of some 450 elk that migrate out of the hills to feed at the Mount Si Golf Course and the publicly owned Meadowbrook Farm, south of the trail on Boalch Road.

The North Bend trailhead, at Fourth Street and Ballarat Avenue, marks the last leg of the trail. Reaching the outskirts of town, the trail begins a barely perceptible grade past rows of blackberry bushes. Passing beneath I-90 and then a short bridge over the rushing South Fork Snoqualmie River, the path begins its winding, 450-foot climb to Rattlesnake Lake over the next 5 miles. Most of the trail is shaded through this section, and it crosses a high trestle over a Boxley Creek tributary.

Signs at the summit point toward Iron Horse State Park, where the trail continues as the John Wayne Pioneer Trail (see page 59). Ahead are Rattlesnake Lake and the Cedar River Education and Conference Center, where visitors can learn more about the area.

CONTACT: kingcounty.gov/recreation/parks/trails/regionaltrailssystem/svt.aspx

DIRECTIONS

To access the trail from McCormick Park in Duvall, take Exit 22 from I-90. At the end of the ramp, head east, and turn right onto SE High Point Way, which becomes Preston–Fall City Road SE after 0.5 mile. After approximately 4 miles, which takes you into Fall City, cross the bridge and take the roundabout north onto WA 203/Fall City–Carnation Road SE. Proceed through Carnation to Duvall; in 14.8 miles, turn left onto NE Stephens St. to reach McCormick Park.

To access the trail from Rattlesnake Lake, take Exit 32 from I-90, and head south on 436th Ave. SE/Cedar Falls Road SE for 3.2 miles to the parking lot at Rattlesnake Lake Recreation Area.

The South Bay Trail is a tourist's dream and a sweet summer spot for locals. The small city of Bellingham, 20 miles from the Canadian border, lies between 10,781-foot Mount Baker and Bellingham Bay and is home to Western Washington University. You'll find easy access to San Juan Island cruises and the Alaska Inside Passage cruise, as well as access to Vancouver, British Columbia.

In the early 1890s, this former line of the Bellingham Bay and Eastern Railroad hauled coal, logs, and lumber from 68 mills to developing West Coast cities. Today, the 2.5-mile trail provides an easy waterfront tour between downtown and the artisan community of Fairhaven, home to many shops, cafés, farmers' markets, and the Fairhaven Village Green, site of weekly outdoor summer movies and music. Two trails—the Interurban and Railroad—connect at either end of the trail.

County
Whatcom

Endpoints
E. Maple St. and Railroad Ave. (Bellingham) to Mill Ave. and 10th St. (Fairhaven)

Mileage
2.5

Roughness Index
2

Surface
Asphalt, Concrete, Crushed Stone

Connecting the city of Bellingham and the artistic neighborhood of Fairhaven, the South Bay Trail puts the classic vistas of Bellingham Bay on display.

South Bay Trail

BELLINGHAM

FINISH

W Holly St

E Chestnut St

W Laurel St

E Maple St

Cornwall Ave

E Laurel St

E Ivy St

N Garden St

High St

Bellingham
Bay

N State St

N Forest St

E Pine St

E Oak St

Forest Ln

N Garden Ter

Morey Ave

WHATCOM COUNTY

Boulevard
Park

P

P

START

P

Bill McDonald Pkwy

15th St

16th St

17th St

20th St

S College Dr

25th St

Adams Ave

Easton Ave

Bennett Ave

Highland Dr

Taylor Ave

P

Taylor Ave

13th St

Douglas Ave

20th St

21st St

Douglas Ave

11th St

SOUTH
HILL

10th St

13th St

Knox Ave

22nd St

23rd St

24th St

P

FINISH

Mill Ave

Mill Ave

9th St

11th St

12th St

14th St

Harris Ave

17th St

18th St

McKenzie Ave

32nd St

4th St

6th St

Donovan Ave

Wilson Ave St

8th St

10th St

Donovan Ave

20th St

N

0   0.125 0.25   0.5 mile

(11)

rails·to·trails
conservancy

You can access the trail in Fairhaven and from anywhere in Boulevard Park. Parking, restrooms, and water are available in the park. A southward journey takes you over the bay via Pattle Point trestle and historic Taylor Dock. A northward trip winds you through Boulevard Park, past a waterfront coffee shop (with Wi-Fi), pocket beaches, and play areas, and across tracks (cross carefully). The linear park trail makes for a peaceful journey among trees and foliage, with intermittent views of the bay, Lummi Island, and the San Juan Islands. You'll pass through the residential outskirts of the restaurant and retail district and arrive downtown, with cafés, a brewery, and other entertainment spots.

The trail ends at Maple Street, just west of Railroad Avenue, where you'll find a farmers' market (open Saturdays), art walks, and the sweet ambience of the area surrounding Western Washington University campus.

CONTACT: cob.org/documents/parks/parks-trails/trail-guide/south_bay.pdf

DIRECTIONS

To access the trail in Fairhaven from I-5, take Exit 250 for WA 11/Old Fairhaven Pkwy. toward Chuckanut Dr. Head west on Connelly Ave./Old Fairhaven Pkwy./WA 11 S, and continue for 1.4 miles. Continue straight onto Donovan Ave., and then continue to the right onto 10th St. for 0.2 mile to Mill Ave. Parking is available near Fairhaven Village Green.

To access the trail in Boulevard Park, take I-5 to Exit 250. Head west on Connelly Ave./Old Fairhaven Pkwy./WA 11 S for 1.5 miles, and turn right at the 12th St. light. In 0.2 mile, bear left onto Finnegan Way, which becomes 11th St. In 0.5 mile, turn left onto Bayview Dr. into Boulevard Park.

To reach the northern terminus at Maple St., take I-5 to Exit 253 heading toward Lakeway Dr. Turn right onto King St. Turn right onto Lakeway Dr. In 0.4 mile, take a slight right onto E. Holly St. After about 0.3 mile, turn left onto Railroad Ave. and look for parking along the side as you head toward Maple St.

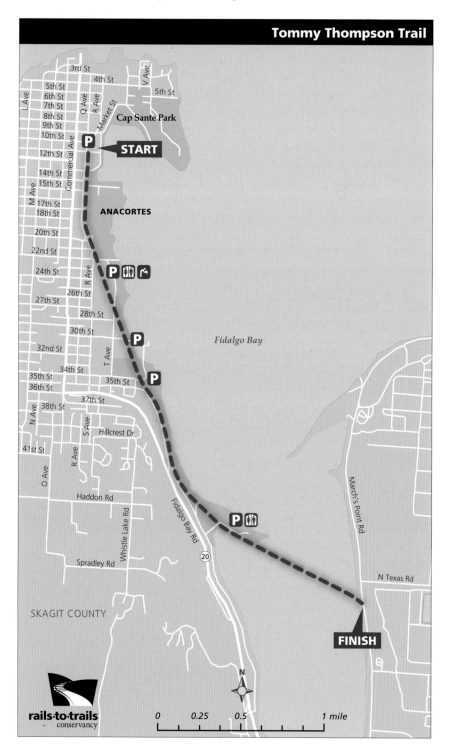

Though relatively short at 3.3 miles, the Tommy Thompson Trail stands tall in the ferry port of Anacortes for its notable 2,000-foot-long paved trestle spanning picturesque Fidalgo Bay.

Enjoyed locally for family outings, sightseeing, and bird-watching, the rail-trail is also significant for its proximity to a Washington State Ferry Terminal (4 miles west of the trail). Those ferries to and from the San Juan Islands or Victoria, British Columbia, often carry bicyclists whose travels include the trail on the first leg of their journeys.

The rail-trail follows the inactive corridor of the short-lived Seattle and Northern Company line, which was built in 1890 when Anacortes boomed as a promised hub of a transcontinental railway. When investors ran out of money, the boom turned to bust. What's more, the railroad realized that a cross-country route from Anacortes

Riding the 2,000-foot trestle across Fidalgo Bay is an excellent way to make your entrance into the city of Anacortes.

County
Skagit

Endpoints
11th St. and Q Ave. to March's Point Road (Anacortes)

Mileage
3.3

Roughness Index
1

Surface
Asphalt

wasn't feasible. The Great Northern Railway bought the short line, built the depot in 1911, and eventually merged into the Burlington Northern Santa Fe Railroad, which discontinued service along the Anacortes branch.

The route is named for Tommy Thompson, a passionate local railroad hobbyist who hand-built the Anacortes railway. He operated the popular six-block narrow-gage railway for some 25 years until his death in 1999.

The tourist train and steam locomotive puffed within a couple blocks of today's northern endpoint for the Tommy Thompson Trail at 11th Street and Q Avenue. That's also just a few blocks from The Depot Arts & Community Center (611 R Avenue) and a block from the Port of Anacortes and waterfront. Heading south, the flat trail continues past boatyards, marinas, and other maritime businesses as it passes trailheads and parking at 22nd, 30th, and 34th Streets.

After that last trailhead, the path rolls along the shoreline below some bluffs and then crosses Fidalgo Bay on the long trestle that connects Weaverling Spit and March's Point. Along the way, visitors are treated to murals, trailside sculptures, and more than a half-dozen turnouts with interpretive signs that describe the local history, economy, flora, and fauna. In that final mile, the forest of firs and madrones gives way to mudflats at low tide. The shallow waters expose eelgrass beds and habitat for salmon, other fish, and marine animals. Snowcapped Mount Baker can be seen in the distance on clear days, while great blue herons and bald eagles fly overhead.

When a mysterious fire damaged the trestle in 2009, local boosters quickly raised the money to repair it. Another local fund-raising effort is under way to complete the Guemes Channel Trail, which would link the Tommy Thompson Trail to the ferry terminal.

CONTACT: skagitbeaches.org/trail-tales-home.html

DIRECTIONS

From I-5, take Exit 230, and turn left onto WA 20 W. After a little more than 14 miles, turn right onto R Ave. Turn right onto 34th St., 30th St., or 22nd St. to find trail parking and trailheads. (A bus stop, water, and restrooms are available at 22nd St. and R Ave.) Continuing north, R Ave. becomes Q Ave., and street parking for the northern endpoint is available in the vicinity of 11th St. (1.5 miles from WA 20). There is no parking at the March's Point Road endpoint.

30 Wallace Falls Railway Trail

Located in the Cascade foothills near the town of Gold Bar, the Wallace Falls Railway Trail (Railroad Grade) climbs 2.5 miles to meet a separate, 1.5-mile riverside ascent to Wallace Falls.

The trail traces the path of wood-fired logging trains, owned by the Great Northern Railroad (GN), which hauled timber to mills and to the GN depot at Gold Bar. Industrialist Friedrich Weyerhaeuser purchased 900,000 acres of surrounding land from GN owner James J. Hill and founded Weyerhaeuser Timber Company. Washington later purchased a portion of the land, and in 1977, Wallace Falls State Park opened to the public.

From the trailhead, you'll quickly reach a fork. (Forking right takes you onto the steep, 1.5-mile Woody Trail, perched above the river.) Forking left allows you to continue on the Wallace Falls Railway Trail, which boasts a

County
Snohomish

Endpoints
Ley Road to Upper Falls in Wallace Falls State Park (north of Gold Bar)

Mileage
3.7

Roughness Index
2

Surface
Dirt, Grass

Blankets of moss and foliage are everywhere you look in the Cascade foothills.

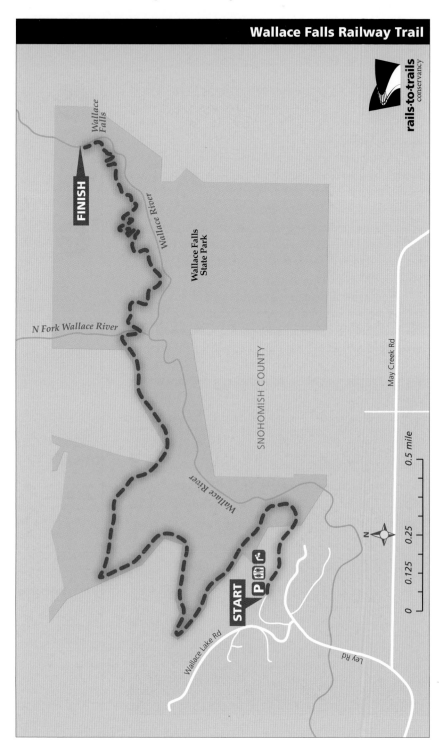

smooth biking surface and more gradual hiking terrain. Broad switchbacks take you through the mossy, wet forest—home to birds and deer, as well as predatory creatures, such as bears and coyotes, that remain largely out of sight.

Staying on the railroad grade, you'll continue past several trails to the steep drop of the North Fork of the Wallace River. Use caution to ensure a safe crossing. At 1.5 miles, a kiosk and a picnic table mark the intersection with a trail that leads to Wallace Lake.

A riverside viewpoint and picnic shelter provides a vista of the Lower Falls, followed shortly by the Middle Falls, the park's highest at 265 feet. Many trail users stop here to avoid the 0.5 mile of steep, short switchbacks to the less dramatic Upper Falls viewpoint at 1,700 (vertical) feet. Beautiful views of the mountains make the descent an enjoyable one.

CONTACT: parks.wa.gov/289/Wallace-Falls

DIRECTIONS

To reach Wallace Falls State Park from I-405, take Exit 23. Follow WA 522 E for 12.9 miles. Take US 2 E for 13.4 miles. Follow signs to the park, and turn left (north) onto First St. (at the park sign). Proceed for 0.4 mile. Turn right onto May Creek Road. Continue a little more than 1 mile to the park and trailhead.

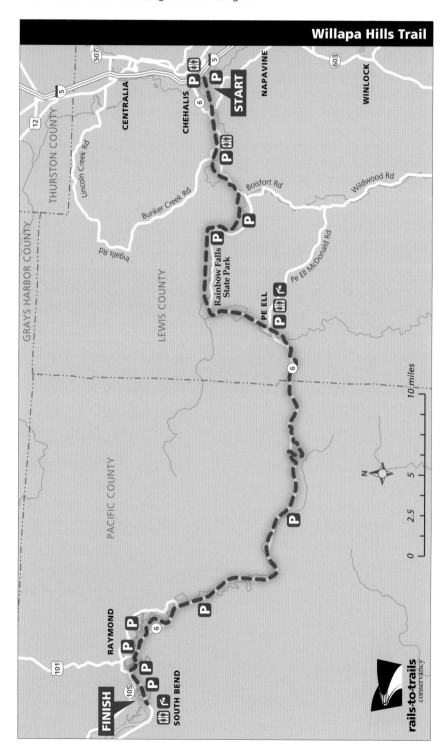

An adventure awaits those who tackle all, or part, of the 56-mile-long Willapa Hills Trail in southwestern Washington. The former Northern Pacific Railway line rolls through remote farm and forestland as it links Chehalis in the east with South Bend on the coast.

The trail boasts inviting, smooth asphalt for 5.3 miles as it leaves Chehalis. Another paved section rolls for 5.2 miles through the coastal towns of Raymond and South Bend on the tidal Willapa River. Sandwiched in between are about 45 miles of trail surface—including packed and loose gravel, ballast, and grass—posing various degrees of difficulty. That middle section features many century-old trestles, some with missing decks, some with missing handrails, and some just missing altogether. Two trestles

The middle section of the Willapa Hills Trail is unpaved, and some sections are quite rugged. Prepare yourself for an adventure!

Counties
Lewis, Pacific

Endpoints
Near end of SW Hillburger Road (Chehalis) to near US 101 and Montana Ave. (South Bend)

Mileage
56

Roughness Index
1–3

Surface
Asphalt, Ballast, Crushed Stone, Grass, Gravel

that were washed out in the 2007 flood—at Spooner Road and Doty-Dryad Road—should be rebuilt and open by late 2015.

The route starts in Chehalis near the tourist train headquarters at the Chehalis-Centralia Railroad & Museum. You'll pass through pastures and small woodlots, and cross two trestles, before reaching a short stretch of gravel to slow down cyclists at a dangerous crossing of WA 6 in Adna. After 2 miles, a 0.2-mile-long trestle with no deck covering the crossbeams marks the end of this section of trail. This trestle will be redecked, and side rails will be added, by the end of 2015.

Beyond, you'll find a packed gravel trail and two more interruptions—construction sites for washed-out trestles at Spooner Road and Dryad—as you pass whitewater in the river and once-thriving lumber mill towns.

The trail deteriorates to mostly loose gravel en route to Pe Ell, a trailhead and old railway town said to be the mispronunciation of an early trapper named Pierre. The next 12 miles feature a winding grade in the Willapa Hills through timber stands of Douglas fir, cedar, and alder. You might spy deer or other wildlife here as you climb and descend a ballast trail held together by grass.

It's back to rough gravel as you return to the valley and pass the small towns of Frances, Lebam (reversed spelling of Mabel, a settler's daughter), and Menlo. A missing trestle just west of Lebam requires a short detour on Robertson Road.

From there, it's nearly 14 more miles of gravel until the path is paved once again as it rolls along the Willapa River on the outskirts of Raymond. The city is known as the Town of Metal People for erecting more than 100 sculptures of animals and people. The route briefly leaves the railroad corridor to avoid a river crossing. It ends on US 101 at a mountain of oyster shells next to the Willapa estuary in South Bend, known as the Oyster Capital of the World.

CONTACT: lewiscountytrails.org

DIRECTIONS

To reach the Chehalis trailhead, take I-5 to Exit 77. Turn west onto W. Main St., and then immediately turn left onto SW Riverside Dr. In 0.5 mile, turn left onto SW Sylvenus St., and then turn right onto SW Hillburger Road in 0.3 mile. At the end, in 0.4 mile, is a county parking lot for the trail; a left turn heads to a state parking lot with toilets and drinking water (Discover Pass required).

To reach the South Bend trailhead from I-5, take Exit 104. Continue on US 101 for 5.5 miles, and keep left to stay on WA 8. In 21 miles, continue straight on US 12. In another 10 miles, take the exit for WA 107/Montesano/Raymond. Turn left onto WA 107 S, and go 8 miles. Turn left onto US 101 S, and travel 21.3 miles. Turn right onto Summit Ave., and park at the trailhead.

Commuters move between the cities of Olympia and Lacey along a former Burlington Northern corridor now known as the Woodland Trail. Connection with the I-5 Trail offers an expanded nonmotorized corridor. The Chehalis Western Trail (see page 25) runs north and south from the midpoint of the Woodland Trail, forming a county network for commuting and recreation.

The Northern Pacific Railroad laid its tracks, which were later purchased by the Burlington Northern, into downtown Olympia in 1891. Service was discontinued, and the right-of-way was acquired for trail construction. The city of Olympia manages the southwestern section of the trail, and Lacey manages the northwestern segment.

The trailhead in Olympia features green architecture, such as a shelter and restroom with solar-tube lighting and a living roof (covered with plants). The parking lot

County
Thurston

Endpoints
Eastside St. SE and Wheeler Ave. SE (Olympia) to Woodland Creek Community Park (Lacey)

Mileage
5

Roughness Index
1

Surface
Asphalt, Gravel

With a trailhead in downtown Olympia, this trail offers immediate access for those who live in the state capital.

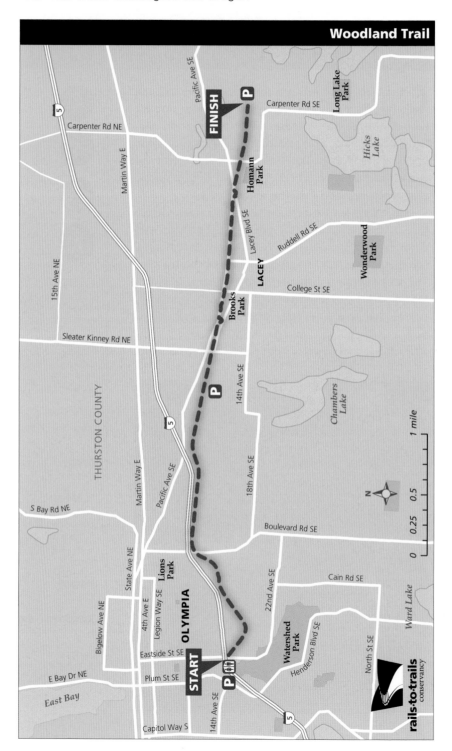

Woodland Trail

comprises porous pavement, and a rain garden filters storm water. From the trailhead, the route runs northeast on a mild uphill grade, intersecting after 2.5 miles with the Chehalis Western Trail. You'll pass benches and more than 12,000 native tree and shrub plantings. At the four-way intersection of the two trails (the Chehalis Western Trail runs both north and south), an access point leads north to Pacific Avenue and a small retail area.

The Lacey segment begins here and parallels busy Pacific Avenue through downtown Lacey, reaching the meadows of Woodland Creek Community Park after 2.2 miles. Two busy traffic circles create safety issues for children and inexperienced riders. Use great caution, as traffic enters quickly and drivers may not see you. Recreational riders may consider continuing on the Chehalis Western Trail.

Once you've passed Carpenter Street, you'll come to the trail's end at Woodland Creek Community Park. Highlights include Woodland Creek, which weaves through the property, as well as Longs Pond (year-round fishing for children age 14 and under), additional trails, and a trestle.

CONTACT: olympiawa.gov/city-services/parks/parks-and-trails/olympia
-woodland-trail or tinyurl.com/woodlandtrail

DIRECTIONS

To reach the Olympia trailhead (1600 Eastside St. SE) from I-5, take Exit 105 toward Port of Olympia. Head north on Plum St. SE. Turn right onto Union Ave. SE; in 0.2 mile, turn right onto Eastside St. SE. The destination will be on your left in 0.4 mile.

Pedestrian- and bicycle-only trailheads are located at Frederick St., Boulevard Road, Pacific Ave., and Dayton St. SE. From the Olympia trailhead, follow Wheeler Ave. SE to the Frederick St. (0.7 mile) and Boulevard Road (0.9 mile) trailheads. The Pacific Ave. trailhead is located off Exit 107 from I-5. From the Boulevard Road trailhead, follow Boulevard Road south for 0.3 mile, and turn left onto 15th Ave. SE/Dayton St. SE. In 0.7 mile, you will reach the trailhead.

To reach the Lacey trailhead at Woodland Creek Community Park, from I-5, take Exit 109. Head east on Martin Way E. Go 1 mile, and turn right onto Carpenter Road SE. After 0.9 mile, turn left onto Pacific Ave. SE, and then turn right into the park.

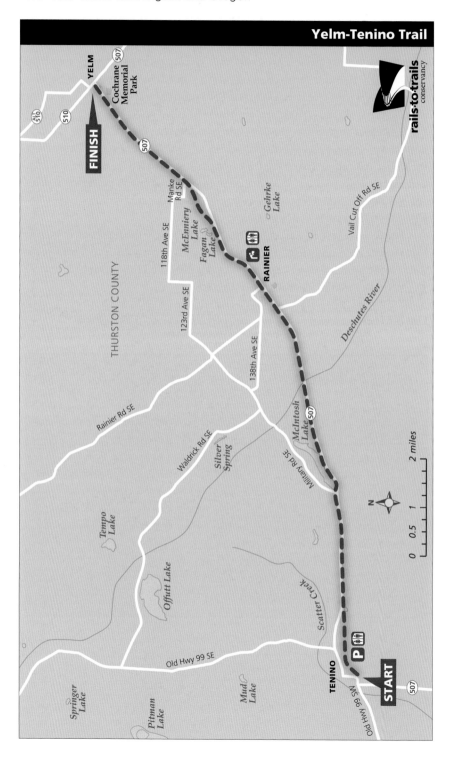

Yelm-Tenino Trail

The 14-mile Yelm-Tenino Trail travels through the rural towns of Yelm, Rainier, and Tenino on a paved route through agricultural areas, forests, and wetlands. Commuters can access Olympia, Lacey, and other areas of Thurston County on a triad of linked trails. The 21.2-mile Chehalis Western Trail (see page 25) intersects the midpoint of the Yelm-Tenino Trail. The Chehalis Western then runs north, connecting with the Woodland Trail (see page 111) and reaching the perimeter of Woodard Bay. The Yelm-Tenino Trail climbs a gentle 320 feet from Tenino to Yelm.

Tenino was the destination of the Northern Pacific Railroad's 65-mile Pacific Division line between Kalama and Tenino as early as 1872. In 1874, a 40-mile line was built through Yelm to Commencement Bay in Tacoma; this line operated as a Burlington Northern line until the

County
Thurston

Endpoints
Crowder Road at Park Ave. (Tenino) to Railroad St. SW (Yelm)

Mileage
14

Roughness Index
1

Surface
Asphalt

A moderate grade, plus a shaded corridor of green, is sure to equal an ideal rail-trail experience.

late 1980s. Tenino, known as the Stone City, built a sandstone depot, now the Tenino Depot Museum, in 1914 along the main line from Portland to Tacoma.

You can start your journey at Tenino City Park, adjacent to a campground. After running past a few homes, a ballpark, and restrooms, the route begins to parallel WA 507. The forested path then crosses Military Road to rise above WA 507. The road is never far, but a swath of fir and maple trees provides a barrier. A historical kiosk precedes 1 mile of scenic forest trail beside McIntosh Lake, where herons come to watch trail users.

At 6.5 miles, you'll reach the intersection to the Chehalis Western Trail. The Rainier trailhead lies just 2 miles farther. The landscape widens as you pass through Wilkowski Park and cross under a trestle. The trail runs closer to the road for the next 5 miles as it approaches Yelm, eventually ending at the trailhead on Railroad Street Southwest.

CONTACT: co.thurston.wa.us/parks/trails-yelm-tenino.htm

DIRECTIONS

To reach the Tenino trailhead from I-5, take Exit 102, Trosper Road SW/toward Black Lake. Head east on Trosper Road SW. In 0.3 mile, turn right onto Capitol Blvd. SE, and go 1.9 miles. Continue on Old Highway 99 SE for 9.1 miles, and turn right at the T-intersection onto Sussex Ave. E/WA 507. Immediately turn left onto S. Ragless St. In 0.1 mile, turn right onto Park Ave. E. Turn left at the entrance to the city park at 309 W. Park Ave.

To reach the Yelm trailhead (behind City Hall on Railroad St. SW) from I-5, take Exit 111/WA 510. Follow WA 510 southeast for 12 miles (making a few turns to remain on WA 510). Turn right onto Railroad St. SW. Find the trail at the corner of Washington St. SW.

The Rainier trailhead is on Centre St. just off WA 507. From I-5, take Exit 109. Head west on Martin Way E, and immediately turn left onto College St. SE/Rainier Road SE. After 13.9 miles, veer right onto Minnesota St. N. In 0.3 mile, turn left onto Binghampton St., and then make an immediate left onto Centre St. N. Trailhead parking is on the left.

A gazebo along the Lower Yakima Valley Pathway (see page 66) offers a welcome resting spot for trail users.

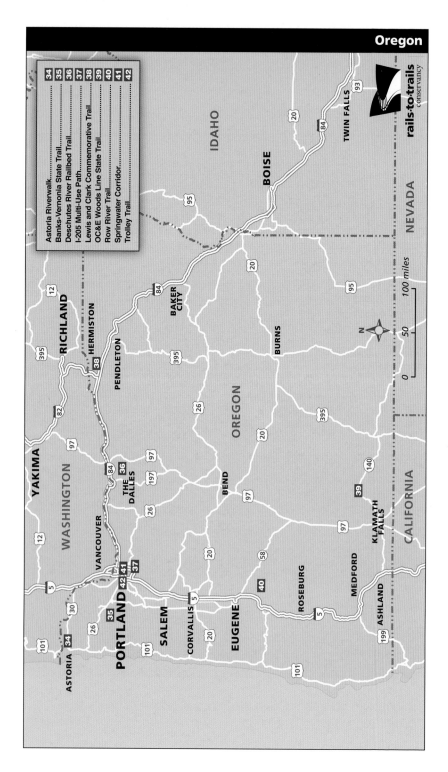

Oregon

rails·to·trails
conservancy

Oregon

From ships and trolleys to birds and sea lions, there is plenty to see along the Astoria Riverwalk.

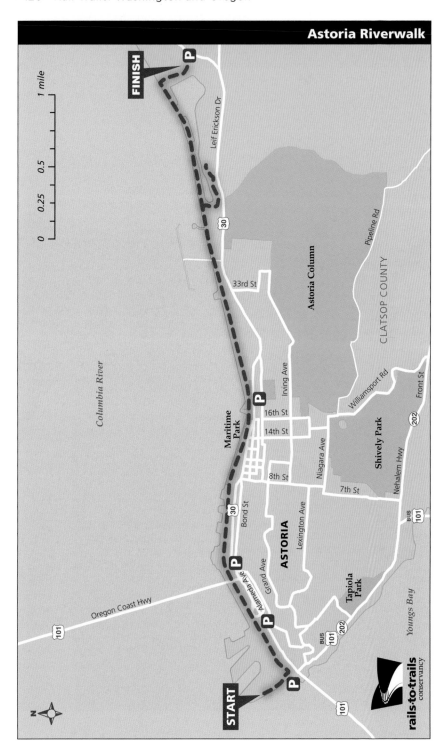

Astoria Riverwalk

The Astoria Riverwalk, also known as the Astoria River Trail, stretches along part of the Astoria & Columbia River Railroad, providing a lively, nonmotorized tour of the city's waterfront. Along the way, you'll find museums, restaurants, breweries, and interpretive kiosks, as well as a 1913 trolley (open March–December) that offers a historical narrative of the area, home to the one of the oldest European American settlements in the West. The shore is also an important site where 20,000 birds may gather each year during fall migration.

The Astoria & Columbia River Railroad completed laying its tracks in the area in 1898, later to be acquired by the Spokane, Portland & Seattle Railway. The railway became popular with weekend tourists heading to the coast. The timber industry kept it running into the early

The Astoria Riverwalk shows off the beauty of the region's historical waterfront.

County
Clatsop

Endpoints
Pier 3 at the Port of Astoria to Lagoon Road (Astoria)

Mileage
6.4

Roughness Index
1

Surface
Asphalt

1990s, and the city's waterfront revitalization effort opened the first trail section in 1995.

You can access the trail almost anywhere along its length, or begin at the western trailhead at the Port of Astoria, home to hundreds of ships. The route takes you under the 4.1-mile Astoria-Megler Bridge, the longest continuous three-span through-truss bridge in North America. Here, you can take in stunning river views, as well as the Maritime Memorial, which pays tribute to the area's seafaring history and locals lost at sea. Beware! The Columbia is as dangerous to ships as it is beautiful to the eye. Since 1846, bar pilots have leapt from tugs (and in modern times, also helicopters) onto ships to guide them across the river's treacherous shifting sandbars at this "Graveyard of the Pacific."

As you make your way east, you'll come to a loading point for these famous pilots. You can also visit a number of nearby shipwrecks; learn more at the world-class Columbia River Maritime Museum at 17th Street. As you continue your journey, you'll pass a chorus of barking sea lions lounging underneath the trestles and basking on the docks at 36th Street. The trail ends at the lagoons near Tongue Point.

CONTACT: tinyurl.com/riverwalkastoria

DIRECTIONS

To get to Astoria, take US 30 west or US 101 north. To reach the Port of Astoria, from US 101, after crossing the bridge, go 0.5 mile on Marine Dr. Or, from US 30, after crossing the John Day River, continue on US 30 for 6.9 miles. Turn north onto Portway St., and take the second left onto Gateway Ave. Parking can be found at the Maritime Memorial (200 W. Marine Dr.) adjacent to the Astoria-Megler Bridge, as well as at the museum and along most streets parallel to the trail.

You'll find a gravel lot at the east end of the trail on Lagoon Road. From US 30, turn north onto 45th St. After 0.2 mile, turn right onto Cedar St. After 0.5 mile, turn left onto 51st St. and make an immediate right onto Birch St., which turns left and becomes 53rd St. and then turns right to become Alder St. Alder St. turns into Lagoon Road, and in less than 0.5 mile after turning onto Birch St., you will see the gravel lot on your left.

Rail access is available to Tongue Point via the Astoria Branch of the Portland & Western Railroad.

The Banks-Vernonia State Trail stretches through the hills (east of the Coast Mountains) between its two namesake towns. The former railroad corridor—once part of the Spokane, Portland & Seattle Railway—hauled timber from mills in Vernonia and Keasey to Portland beginning in the 1920s until 1957. For five years during the 1960s, the line was used for passenger excursions. Oregon Parks and Recreation gained official ownership of the right-of-way in 1990.

Thirteen bridges, as well as two 700-foot-long, 80-foot-high railroad trestles at Buxton and Horseshoe, offer amazing views. The gentle grade (in all but one area) provides beautiful scenes of the Coast Range from forested hills, as well as access to side trails displaying railroad relics and to a number of rivers and creeks. A variety of flora and fauna also populates the trail. Most of the route consists of an

The Buxton Trestle near mile 6 is one of the many things to look forward to on the Banks-Vernonia State Trail.

Counties
Columbia, Washington

Endpoints
NW Banks Road and NW Sellers Road (Banks) to Anderson Park at Jefferson Ave. (Vernonia)

Mileage
21

Roughness Index
1

Surface
Asphalt

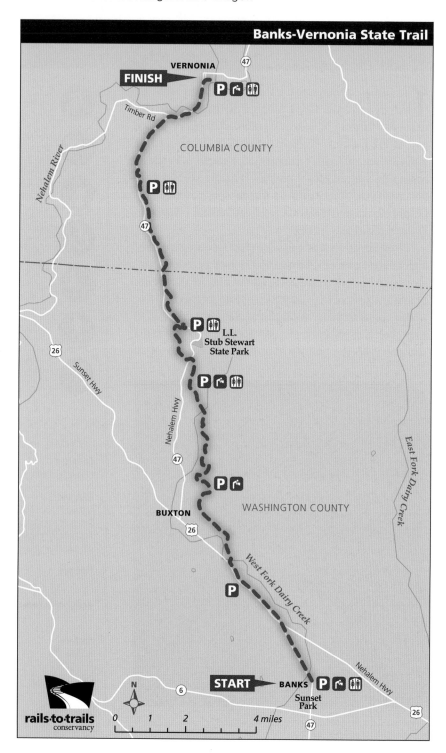

Banks-Vernonia State Trail

8-foot-wide hiking and bicycling trail paralleled by a 4-foot-wide horse trail. The trail rises from Banks to Vernonia on an average 2% to 5% grade. One exception is the Horseshoe Trestle bypass, which switchbacks up 700 feet and descends 300 feet at Tophill.

Equestrians will find ADA-accessible loading platforms and hitching posts at several trailheads. Please use caution cycling on any speedy downhill shots. Yield to horses, and be visible or audible when approaching.

From Banks, enjoy a gentle 5-mile incline—good for families—through pastoral farmland. The grade steepens a bit on mostly wide and sweeping switchbacks as you approach the Buxton trailhead in a canopy of trees. The Horseshoe Trestle was half-destroyed by fire, but bikers and hikers can cross the curving 700 feet of the restored Buxton Trestle at about mile 6. A ground-level equestrian bypass crosses Mendenhall Creek.

The route continues to the Buxton trailhead, where you can picnic and wander interpretive trails. You'll then pass through L. L. Stub Stewart State Park, a 1,700-acre full-service state park and campground. Just before reaching the Tophill trailhead at mile 12, the route descends into short, steep switchbacks across Nehalem Highway, bypassing the Horseshoe Trestle, and then climbs back to the trailhead.

After the Beaver Creek trailhead at mile 17, the path emerges from the woods and hugs the highway for a gentle descent into Vernonia. Prepare for a few bumpy spots and tight turns near Vernonia. The route officially ends at Anderson Park, just blocks from downtown Vernonia, but the pavement continues for a couple more miles to Mill Pond/Vernonia Lake. Vernonia offers shops, galleries, and a museum.

CONTACT: tinyurl.com/banksstatetrl

DIRECTIONS

You can access the trail in Vernonia, Buxton, Manning, or Banks. The route passes through L. L. Stub Stewart State Park; however, day-use parking is not easily accessible from here, aside from a loading zone at the trail crossing of the park road.

The Banks trailhead provides the best parking, as well as restrooms and drinking water. From Portland, drive west on US 26 for about 21 miles. Go about 0.5 mile past OR 6 (NW Wilson River Hwy.), and turn left onto NW Banks Road. In 1.7 miles, look for the lot at the bottom of a steep hill near NW Sellers Road.

To reach the Vernonia trailhead, from Portland, drive west on US 26 about 28 miles. Make a slight right onto OR 47 N (Nehalem Hwy.), and go 14.4 miles, looking for signs for Vernonia/Clatskanie. Turn right onto Bridge St. Go 0.2 mile, and turn right (the third right) onto Jefferson Ave. The trailhead will be on the left after 0.2 mile.

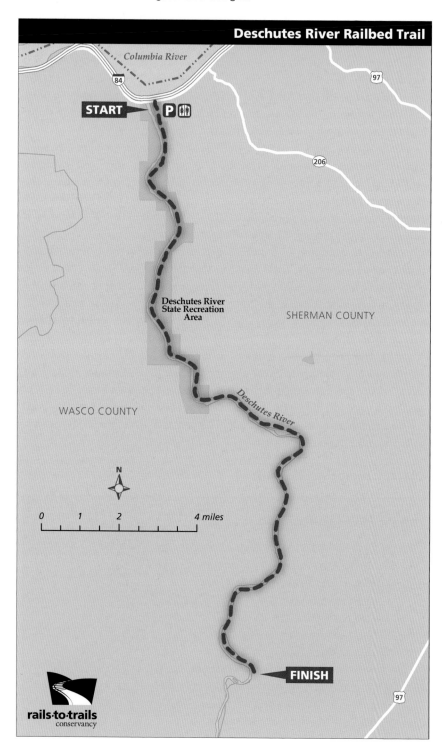

36 Deschutes River Railbed Trail

Whitewater rafters, anglers, kayakers, horseback riders, hikers, and mountain bikers are all drawn to the beauty, wildlife, and history of the Lower Deschutes River, a designated national Wild and Scenic River. The Deschutes River Railbed Trail extends from the shaded camping and family river activities of Deschutes River State Recreation Area into a rare, remote, and scenic river canyon.

You should expect intense heat in the canyon; snacks, liters of insulated water, and hats are recommended. A spring jaunt in moderate weather highlights lupines and other wildflowers—a perfect renewal from the rainy northwest winters. Equestrians may request a trail reservation from March to June.

Caution: The route is dotted with tire-slicing puncture vine, which is cleared by rangers. Bikers should carry tube sealant, along with a patch kit or extra tubes. If you

The Deschutes River Railbed Trail near Bend showcases a dramatic desert canyon region in central Oregon.

County
Sherman

Endpoints
Deschutes River State Recreation Area at OR 206/Biggs-Rufus Hwy. (Wasco) to near Macks Canyon Campground (Grass Valley)

Mileage
17

Roughness Index
2

Surface
Dirt, Gravel

take a side trail, be alert: Grasses may hide rattlers and bull snakes, as well as nestling fawns and ticks. If you leave the wide-open path, consider gaiters or pants tucked into socks.

The trains that used to roll by across the river were built during a turbulent, political east–west clash, when two railroad companies fought from 1908 to 1911 to dominate the route from the mouth of the Columbia River to Bend. The Des Chutes Railroad, where you stand, extended 95 miles to Metolius, while BNSF Railway now owns the 156 miles of the competing Oregon Trunk.

Begin your journey from the state recreation area trailhead, located uphill via a short, narrow pathway. Watch for western meadowlarks, ospreys, doves, golden eagles, herons, and the distinctive black on white of magpies.

At 3.5 miles, you'll approach a patch of shade trees, as well as a trail to the river (with picnic tables and a toilet). Horse troughs and hitching posts begin at 4.5 miles, accompanied by the first of several renovated boxcars providing shelter and history. Along the way, you'll also pass a small trestle and a rock wall built by Chinese railroad workers. A toilet and boxcar at mile 8 offer a good spot for a river swim and respite from the sun. Cottonwood trees planted for shade and grains planted by rangers attract pheasants, quail, chukars, foraging deer, and elk.

Ten miles into the route, the canyon widens and flattens under towering rock formations beside a remnant of a river bridge. The horse path ends at the old Harris Ranch and railroad water tower at mile 11, where many hikers and bikers also turn back.

The bike trail ends at mile 17, as does an accommodating hike. The trail continues 7 rugged miles to Macks Canyon Campground, going up and down the canyon walls once traversed by trestles.

CONTACT: tinyurl.com/deschutesriversra

DIRECTIONS

From The Dalles, head east on I-84/US 30 to Exit 97. Take a right and then an immediate left. Follow OR 206/Celilo-Wasco Hwy. for 3 miles to the Deschutes River State Recreation Area, on your right, just past the Deschutes River Bridge.

If you're heading west on I-84/US 30, take Exit 104. Turn left, and then make an immediate right onto Biggs-Rufus Hwy. Continue for 4.4 miles, and turn left into the Deschutes River State Recreation Area.

Park at the end of the park road. Follow a sign up a steep narrow path to the Railbed Trail.

The I-205 Multi-Use Path spans 18.5 miles through five cities and 15 neighborhoods along I-205 and the TriMet MAX Green Line light rail service. In addition, it joins with the 21.5-mile Springwater Corridor (see page 142), making it an important commuting connection in the greater Portland area. Extending from the northern edge of the Columbia River in Vancouver, Washington, to Gladstone, Oregon, the trail and its amenities—including public art, topiary, wayfinding signage, and, in 2011, 5,000 new trees and shrubs—attract thousands of cyclists and pedestrians each day. The state of Oregon first constructed the trail in the 1980s to improve biking and walking connections between neighborhoods, as well as between commercial and public destinations. The Oregon Department of Transportation reopened the entire route in 2011 after closing sections of it to

Counties
Clackamas, Multnomah

Endpoints
I-205 and Lewis and Clark Hwy./WA 14 (Vancouver, WA) to SE 82nd Dr. (Clackamas, OR); OR 224 and I-205 to 82nd Dr. (Gladstone, OR); S. Washington St. at S. Pope Ln. to Main St. (Gladstone, OR); McLoughlin Blvd./OR 99E and Main St. to 10th St. (Oregon City, OR)

Mileage
18.5

Roughness Index
1

Surface
Asphalt

This urban multiuse path connects communities from Vancouver, Washington, to Gladstone, Oregon.

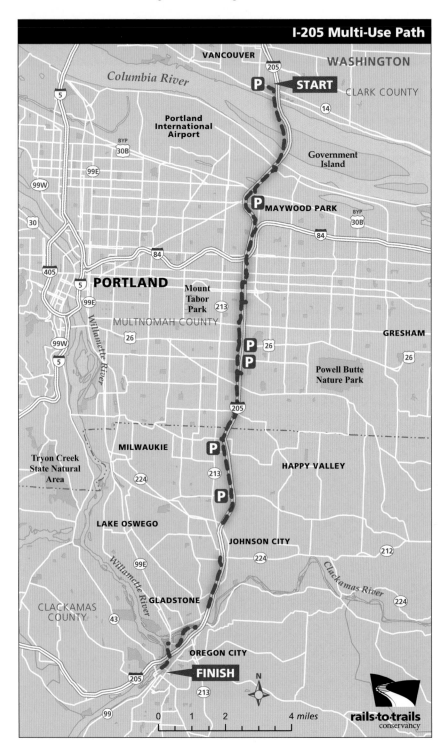

implement a number of enhancements to make it more commuter friendly, such as the installation of new overhead lighting.

Bike routes and bike lanes connect several trail gaps. At I-205 and OR 224/ Milwaukee Expressway (also Southeast 82nd Drive), the trail transitions to bike lanes on Southeast 82nd Drive. You can regain the main trail at OR 212/224. The path ends at the Gladstone interchange, which is just north of Oregon City and High Rocks State Park. The route continues on road to Oregon City via Agnes and Main Streets. Be aware that the tunnel does not have bike lanes.

The trail starts from the north at 23rd Street in Vancouver and runs south to cross the I-205 Bridge. It passes over Government Island, which—reachable only by boat—is known for its great blue heron colony and its state recreation area's primitive camping and beaches. The interior of the island is off-limits to the public.

As you continue south, you'll pass Marine Drive, the Sandy Boulevard trailhead, the Gateway Transit Center, and Powell Boulevard. Eventually, you'll intersect with the Springwater Corridor and then Southeast Johnson Creek Boulevard, passing near Clackamas Town Center and Clackamas Promenade before ending in Gladstone. Heading south from Clackamas Town Center, the pathway crosses Sunnyside Road and Sunnybrook Boulevard, detouring after 1.4 miles onto a bike lane on Southeast 82nd Drive.

You'll return by turning left at Carver Road and, after 0.8 mile, crossing over the freeway to the path. Less than 2 miles farther south, the trail stops at Southeast 82nd Drive and the I-205 Gladstone interchange.

Two more short, disconnected sections of trail are located south of the Clackamas River on the outskirts of Oregon City.

CONTACT: oregon.gov/ODOT/HWY/REGION1/pages/i205_mup/index.aspx

DIRECTIONS

To reach the northern endpoint in Vancouver, WA, take I-205 to Exit 27. Head west on WA 14, and go 1.5 miles to Exit 4. Take a left onto S. Leiser Road, and then take another left to head east on WA 14. After 0.7 mile, take Exit 5, and turn right (south) onto SE Ellsworth Road. Immediately turn left (east) onto 23rd St., and drive to the end.

The Columbia Springs education center is another starting point. To reach the center, pass 23rd St., and take the next left onto SE Evergreen Hwy. Go 0.8 mile, and Columbia Springs will be on your left.

In Portland, access the trail at various transit locations and commuter lots, including the commuter lot along NE Sandy Blvd. at 96th Ave. near I-205 (Exit 23) in Sumner, as well as the Gateway Transit Center at NE 99th Ave. and NE Pacific St. (Exit 21 from I-205) behind Clackamas Town Center. Go to **trimet.org** for details and interactive maps of the MAX Green Line.

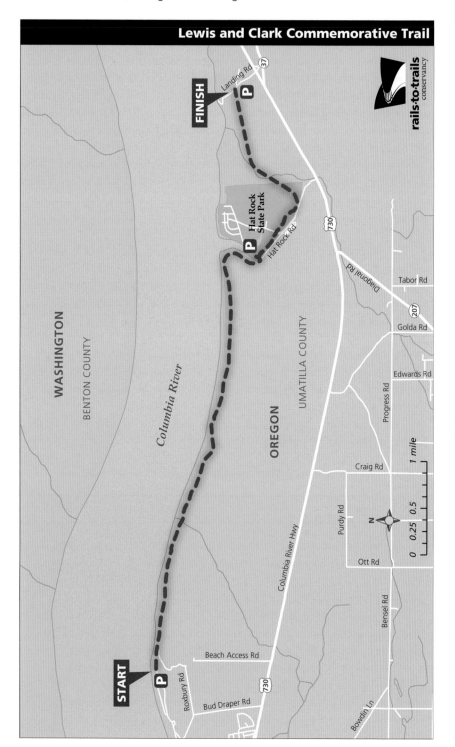

This segment of the historic Lewis and Clark Trail traverses cliffs perched above the Columbia River in the Oregon desert. The fairly flat trail, steep and sandy in sections, gathers the rural treasures of McNary Beach Park, the Columbia River, Hat Rock State Park, and Warehouse Beach Recreation Area. The sun bears down on the sagebrush, and you'll want to make sure to bring adequate water, sunscreen, and a hat. Hiking and horse travel are most common on the trail; mountain bikers will likely dismount through sandy and ungraded sections.

Umatilla is at the southern tip of the I-82 bridge that crosses the vast Columbia River into Washington wine country, also home of the Lower Yakima Valley Pathway. Invisible are miles of the Oregon-Washington Railroad and Navigation Company (OWR&N) and the towns flooded by McNary Dam construction in 1953. Sacrificed

Imagine life before the McNary Dam; towns now submerged by Lake Wallula once populated the banks of the Columbia River.

County
Umatilla

Endpoints
McNary Beach on Beach Access Road to Warehouse Beach on Landing Road (Hermiston)

Mileage
7.3

Roughness Index
3

Surface
Gravel

to rescue the critical trade route of the mighty Columbia from the unrelenting Umatilla rapids, these ghosts now lie under the 64-mile-long Lake Wallula.

This OWR&N division of Union Pacific was rebuilt in a location less vulnerable to the previous years of rockfall and avalanches, which had shoved railcars into the river since the railroad was constructed in the late 1800s.

Starting from the grassy riverfront of McNary Beach Park, a flat trail climbs to a scenic, steep riverbank at 1 mile. Stay high at the fork. The path again flattens on the approach to Hat Rock State Park as stunning views appear of inlets, basalt formations, and cliff-top homes. Boats cruise by, and you can hear the metallic rustle of cheatgrass and bunchgrass. Eagles and hawks soar above.

Desert browns and yellows become bright green as you enter Hat Rock State Park, where willow trees and flowers encircle a pond enjoyed by geese and ducks. A bridge crosses the inlet to open desert trails. Hat Rock towers above the anglers waiting on the banks of the inlet and pond for steelhead and rainbow trout, walleye, and sturgeon.

You'll continue 1.6 miles past the east edge of the park on a relatively level railroad bed to end at Warehouse Beach Recreation Area. Explore all this sunny riverside park has to offer before heading to wine tastings on the Lower Yakima Valley Pathway. Note that only Hat Rock State Park allows pets.

CONTACT: tinyurl.com/hatrock or tinyurl.com/lewisclarkcommtrail

DIRECTIONS

Find the western point, McNary Beach Park, 3 miles east of Umatilla on US 730. Take I-82 to Exit 1. Turn east onto US 730/Columbia River Hwy., and go 2.7 miles. Turn north (left) onto Beach Access Road, and follow it to the end, 1.7 miles. No pets are allowed.

To reach Hat Rock State Park, take US 730 7.9 miles from I-82. Turn north (left) onto Hat Rock State Park Road, and go 1.2 miles. There is no horse parking here.

Warehouse Park, the eastern terminus (with horse trailer lot), can be found 9.1 miles east of the Umatilla exit from I-82. From US 730, bear right onto OR 37 and then left onto Landing Road. This lot has the best equestrian parking but does not allow pets.

39 OC&E Woods Line State Trail

One of the longest rail-trails in the country, the OC&E Woods Line State Trail stretches 109.9 miles through south-central Oregon. The route comprises two rail lines that once supported the region's timber industry: the former Oregon, California & Eastern Railway, also known as the Klamath Falls Municipal Railway, which extended from Klamath Falls to Bly (now the main line of the trail), and the old Weyerhaeuser Woods Line, which connected to the OC&E at Beatty and ran to a point just north of Sycan Marsh. The Southern Pacific and Great Northern Railroads managed the OC&E from the mid-1920s to 1975, at which time Weyerhaeuser took over operations for the line. The rail line saw its decline in the 1980s; in 1992, the line was railbanked and handed over to Oregon Parks and Recreation.

A good place to begin your journey is the OC&E Woods Line State Trail's western terminus in Klamath

Counties
Klamath, Lake

Endpoints
Washburn Way south of S. Sixth St. (Klamath Falls) to Thompson Reservoir (Summer Lake)

Mileage
109.9

Roughness Index
2–3

Surface
Asphalt, Ballast, Cinder, Dirt, Gravel, Wood Chips

There are some backcountry sections along the OC&E Woods Line State Trail, so be prepared for stretches without road or water access.

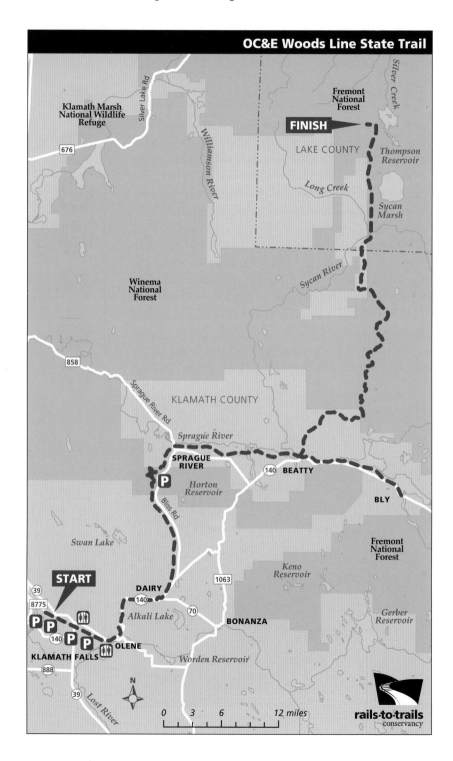

OC&E Woods Line State Trail

Falls, the largest community along the route. From here, you'll travel an 8-mile paved section that passes through residential neighborhoods and open countryside to Olene (be sure to close any gates through which you pass). This part of the route offers beautiful views of Mount Shasta, Poe Valley, and Lost River. The remainder of the trail is unpaved, with surfaces varying from hard-packed to sandy, to rocky, to ranchland, and hilly; this part of the path is well suited for wide-tired bicycles, cross-country skis, and horses. From Olene, the trail heads northeast through quiet pastoral lands with views of mountains in the distance, reaching Beatty after about 40 miles.

Before reaching Dairy, you'll pass through Swede's Cut (at 13.5 miles) and Pine Flat. The trail then heads around Bly Mountain via Switchback Hill—a delightfully scenic backcountry section—and then drops down into the fertile Sprague River Valley. The double switchback—which allowed trains to be split so they could manage the grade—was reportedly the last operating switchback of its kind in the United States.

Note: Water is not available on the trail; you can find convenience stores in Olene, Dairy, Sprague River, Beatty, and Bly. Keep in mind that Dairy (at mile 18) is your last opportunity to buy food or water until you reach Sprague River at mile 35. You'll find cafés in Dairy, Sprague River, Beatty, and Bly.

The Woods Line splits north at Beatty, passing through rocky terrain and the nice backcountry of Fremont National Forest to Sycan Marsh (a great place for bird-watching), where you'll find the northern trailhead. The trail then extends to its endpoint at Thompson Reservoir, where camping and boating are available, as well as access to water and restrooms. The main line continues to the quiet town of Bly (east).

For trout fishing, try Five Mile Creek at Woods Line mile 10. At Woods Line mile 27, you'll come across the Merritt Creek Trestle, which measures 400 feet long and 50 feet high.

Use maps for backcountry sections; signage may not be clear in certain areas. During decent snow years, certain sections offer good cross-country skiing through beautiful forests.

CONTACT: oregonstateparks.org/park_230.php

DIRECTIONS

To reach the Klamath Falls trailhead from I-5, take Exit 747/Weed, and follow US 97 north for 70.4 miles to OR 140/OR 66. Or, take Exit 14/Ashland, and follow OR 66 for 57.9 miles to Klamath Falls. Continue straight (east) onto OR 140 (Klamath Falls–Lakeview Hwy.) for 3.5 miles. Turn left onto Altamont Dr., and go 2.2 miles. Turn left onto Crosby Ave., and look for parking on the right.

Parking is also available at Wiard Park, which has restrooms. From the intersection of OR 66/OR 140 and US 97, take OR 140 east for 4.7 miles, and turn left onto Homedale Road. After 1.5 miles, turn left onto Walton Dr., and then take a right onto Wiard St. after 0.3 mile. Wiard Park is on the left.

From the intersection of OR 66/OR 140 and US 97, take OR 140 east for 6 miles, and turn left onto OR 140/OR 39. The trail crosses the road at 1.4 miles.

To reach the eastern trailhead in Bly from the intersection of OR 66/OR 140 and US 97, follow OR 140 east 55.9 miles (including a short stint on OR 140/OR 39 north) to Bly. Turn right onto Edler St. From US 395 in Lakeview, take OR 140 west for 42.4 miles, and turn left onto Edler St. After 1.4 miles, turn left onto Gerber Ranch Road. After 0.5 mile, turn left onto a dirt road. The trailhead is 0.8 mile ahead.

Other trailheads include Pine Grove, which has restrooms; Switchback, within Fremont National Forest, which offers restrooms and camping; Sycan Siding; and Horse Glade, which also has restrooms.

The Row River Trail is part of the Covered Bridges Scenic Bikeway. Small-town charm, a lake at the foot of the Cascades, and a mostly flat path escort you past Dorena Dam and historic covered bridges. Lane County has more covered bridges than any county west of the Mississippi River.

The trail follows the route of the former Oregon Pacific & Eastern Railroad line, running along the scenic shore of the Row River and Dorena Reservoir and paralleling Row River Road for most of the way. Nearby, you'll find quaint covered bridges and the historic Bohemia mining area. The 3-mile section of trail from Cottage Grove to the Mosby Creek trailhead is managed by the city of Cottage Grove, while the remainder of the trail is managed by the Bureau of Land Management. Cottage Grove has a downtown commercial historic district listed on the National Register of Historic Places.

County
Lane

Endpoints
E. Main St. and S. 10th St.
(Cottage Grove) to Brice
Creek Road (Culp Creek)

Mileage
17

Roughness Index
1

Surface
Asphalt

Over the creek, past the river, and skirting the reservoir—there is a common undercurrent along the Row River Trail.

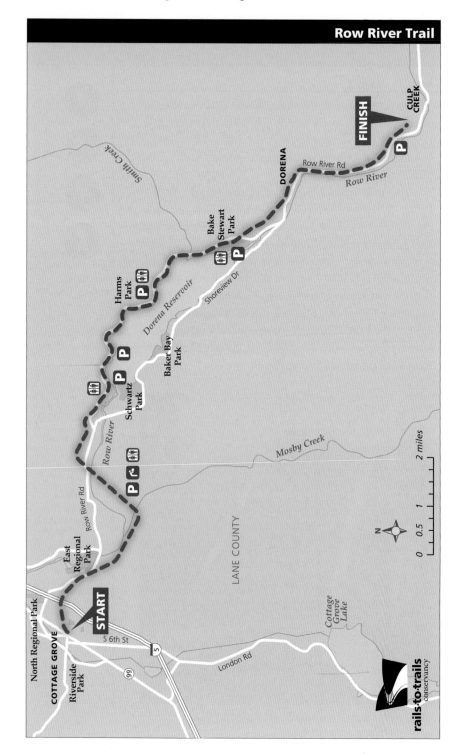

Row River Trail

The Willamette Valley was one of the great farming areas of the 1880s. In the early part of the 20th century, the area relied on the "Old Slow and Easy," more formally known as the Oregon & Southeastern Railroad, to transport goods and people from Cottage Grove to Disston, just past Culp Creek.

From the Cottage Grove trailhead, 3 city miles deliver you to the beautiful Mosby Creek trailhead. After another 3.5 miles, you'll arrive at Dorena Dam, which prevents the flooding of towns downstream. You'll pass Row Point, which displays the colorful, protected remnants of the native prairie, eventually reaching Harms Park Trestle—featured in the movies *Emperor of the North* and *Stand by Me.*

Smith Creek provides habitats for a host of flora and fauna and was once the site of an early settler's orchard; you'll see the remains below Smith Creek Bridge. You'll then pass through post-dam Dorena before completing your tour at Culp Creek—1 of more than 20 early-1900s mill towns that popped up along Row River, sprouting from the short-line railroad from Cottage Grove to the Umpqua National Forest.

CONTACT: tinyurl.com/rowriver

DIRECTIONS

To reach the western trailhead, from I-5 in Cottage Grove, take Exit 174 toward Dorena Lake. Keep right at the exit ramp, following signs for the city center, and merge onto E. Cottage Grove Con. After 0.6 mile, turn left on OR 99, and go 0.7 mile. Turn left onto Main St.; the trailhead will be on the left.

To start outside the city at the Mosby Creek trailhead, from I-5, turn left (east) off the Exit 174 ramp onto Row River Road. Drive 0.7 mile east on Row River Road. Turn right onto Currin Conn Road. Immediately afterward, turn left onto Mosby Creek Road. Go 2 miles southeast on Mosby Creek Road, and then turn left onto Layng Road. Take a quick left into the parking lot. Parking is also provided at smaller trailheads along the way, including Culp Creek.

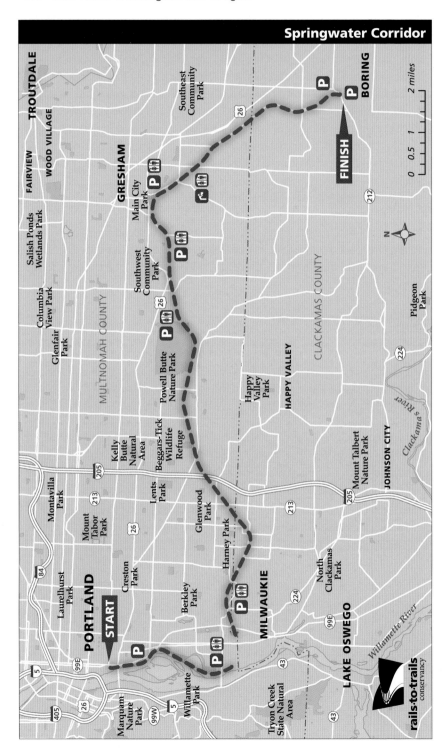

The Springwater Corridor comprises the southeast segment of the 40-Mile Loop regional trail system encircling the greater Portland area. The origins of the Loop come from a 1904 proposal by visionary landscape architects, the Olmsted brothers, who—during the planning process for Portland's Lewis and Clark Centennial Exposition—put forth a plan for a 40-mile system of parks and greenways connected by boulevards. Today, the family-friendly Springwater Corridor follows the banks of the Willamette River from downtown Portland to Johnson Creek and then parallels Johnson Creek through neighborhoods, industrial districts, park refuges, and

Counties
Clackamas, Multnomah

Endpoints
SE Fourth Ave. and SE Ivon St. (Portland) to Clackamas-Boring Hwy. No. 174/OR 212 and SE Richey Road (Boring)

Mileage
21.5

Roughness Index
1

Surface
Asphalt

The Springwater Corridor has been many things during its lifetime. Now, it serves as a vital recreation and transportation corridor for residents and visitors in the Portland area.

wetlands—eventually ending in the town of Boring. Portland's light rail and city buses enhance options and ease of travel along the route's length.

The history of the trail stretches back to the early 1900s, when a rail line was built to bring people, produce, and timber from areas south and east of Portland into the growing metropolis. Known variously as the Portland Traction Company Line, the Cazadero Line, or the Bellrose Line, the railroad finally adopted the name Springwater Division Line, though neither the railroad nor the trail that bears the town's name ever reached this small community. In 1990, Portland bought the railroad corridor, which had ceased its passenger service in 1958 and its freight and timber hauling in the 1980s. The multiuse trail opened in 1996.

For a recreational tour, start at the Johnson Creek Boulevard trailhead; it provides ease of parking and avoids the on-road section between Ninth and 19th Avenues. Sellwood Riverfront Park is an alternate start point and worth a visit if you don't mind this bit of road section. The downtown start at Southeast Fourth Avenue and Southeast Ivon Street is another option. To avoid an industrial section from mile 8, which is not well traveled during the week or at night, choose the trailhead east of the I-205 Multi-Use Path at Flavel Street.

The Johnson Creek Boulevard trailhead sits at mile 6. If you backtrack a bit to cross the creek, you'll find a natural area. At mile 9, you'll cross the I-205 Multi-Use Path (see page 129) and eventually reach Southeast 111th Avenue and Beggars-Tick Wildlife Refuge. A right onto Southeast 122nd Avenue leads to the 17-acre Leach Botanical Garden, which boasts more than 2,000 plant species. Just a little farther along is the 612-acre Powell Butte Nature Park, offering meadows, forests, and mammal and bird habitats enjoyed by hikers, mountain bikers, and horseback riders.

The next part of the trail leads you through a hilly area toward the Cascade foothills. Take in the grandeur of Mount Hood, which stands at 11,240 feet. The trail then crosses Johnson Creek (mile 13)—a serene spot (with covered benches) to rest your feet and relax. Farther along, you'll reach Linnemann Station, after which you'll intersect with the 3-mile Gresham Fairview Trail, which runs north and will eventually connect with Marine Drive in Portland. The path leads to Gresham's Main City Park at mile 16. If you exit through the park to Powell Boulevard, you can explore Gresham's pedestrian walkway in the shadow of Mount Hood. MAX, Portland's light rail, is accessible nearby. The trail ends 5 miles farther at OR 212 in Boring.

CONTACT: portlandoregon.gov/parks/finder

DIRECTIONS

Access to the trail is available at many locations, including the I-205 Multi-Use Path. To reach the Johnson Creek Blvd. trailhead, from I-205, take Exit 16 and go east on SE Johnson Creek Blvd. for 2.2 miles. Turn left to stay on Johnson Creek Blvd., and the trailhead is just past Johnson Creek on your right.

To reach the Boring trailhead at 28000 SE Dee St., from Gresham, head west-southwest on US 26 for 3.8 miles. Turn left onto SE Stone Road, and after 0.5 mile, take a right onto SE 282nd Ave. Go 2 miles, and turn right onto OR 212. Take an immediate right onto SE Dee St., and parking will be on the left. From I-205, take Exit 14. Go east on SE Sunnyside Road for 5.8 miles. Turn left onto OR 212, and follow it for 4.5 miles. Turn left onto SE Dee St., and parking will be on the left.

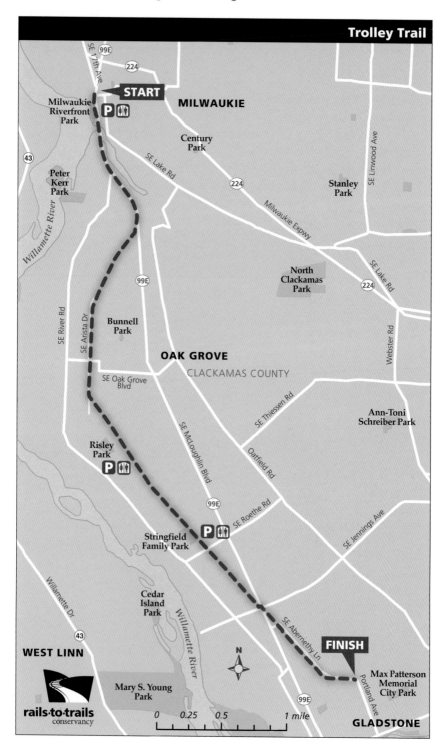

The Trolley Trail follows the Portland Traction Company's Oregon City Line streetcar right-of-way, serving Portland's metro area, that ran between Milwaukie and Gladstone from 1893 until 1968.

Currently, 6 miles of the trail are complete. The trail is part of a planned 20-mile loop that will connect Portland, Milwaukie, Gladstone, Oregon City, and Gresham—linking schools, parks, commercial districts, and historical sites along the way. Metro and the North Clackamas Parks & Recreation District (NCPRD) purchased the right-of-way in December 2001. Developed in 2012, the trail completes a missing link in Metro's regional trail system. It presently reaches bike lanes in Milwaukie and Gladstone and will eventually link to both the Springwater Corridor and the I-205 Multi-Use Path.

Whether you stroll solo, frolic with friends, or share the journey with loved ones, the Trolley Trail is the perfect spot to recharge.

County
Clackamas

Endpoints
SE Harrison St. at OR 99E/SE McLoughlin Blvd. (Milwaukie) to Portland Ave. at Abernethy Ln. (Gladstone)

Mileage
6

Roughness Index
1

Surface
Asphalt

Milwaukie Riverfront Park on the Willamette River provides a great starting point. Summer Sundays bring the farmers' market just across the street. As you make your way along the trail, wide corridors of trees and grass buffer you from city streets; you may encounter a host of wildlife, including opossums, beavers, great blue herons, green herons, and Western screech-owls.

On either side of the length of the trail, you'll find historic homes claiming many styles of architecture, including Arts & Crafts, Craftsman, Queen Anne, Colonial Revival, and more. Just past Courtney Road to your left, the Elizabeth Heitkamper House, completed in 1888, is the largest and most prominent example of Queen Anne–Vernacular style in north Clackamas County.

The trail passes through the playgrounds and nature areas of Stringfield Park, eventually ending at East Jersey Street in Gladstone. After this point, you'll find intermittent bike lanes and sidewalks.

In the next couple of years, the trail will extend 1 mile north along Southeast 17th Avenue to reach the Springwater Corridor. Currently, this section of street riding is used by seasoned commuters and is not recommended for families or trail riders.

CONTACT: ncprd.com/parks/trolley-trail or hhpr.com/trolleytrail

DIRECTIONS

To reach Milwaukie Riverfront Park from downtown Portland, take OR 99E (which later becomes SE McLoughlin Blvd.) about 6 miles south to SE Jefferson St. You'll find a large, paved lot situated by the river on your right.

To reach the Stringfield Park trailhead (mid-trail, 3614 SE Naef Road), from downtown Portland, take OR 99E (which later becomes SE McLoughlin Blvd.) about 9 miles south, and turn left onto SE Naef Road. Stringfield Park will be on your left.

Street parking is available at the trail's southern endpoint at E. Jersey St. and Portland Ave. in Gladstone. Take I-205 to Exit 11, and head west on 82nd Dr. for 0.3 mile. Turn right onto E. Arlington St., and go 0.5 mile. Turn right onto Portland Ave., and in 0.4 mile, you will arrive at the trailhead.

Index

Photo Credits

Page iii: Jessie H. Lin; *page x:* Lauren Kailian; *page 7:* Jessie H. Lin; *page 9:* CF Hsieh; *page 11:* Bryce Hall; *page 15:* Eckart Schmidt; *pages 19 and 21:* Barbara Richey/Rails-to-Trails Conservancy; *page 25:* Karl Wirsing; *page 29:* Mia Barbera; *page 31:* Cowiche Canyon Conservatory; *pages 35 and 37:* Barbara Richey/Rails-to-Trails Conservancy; *page 41:* Karen Jurasin; *pages 43 and 47:* Barbara Richey/Rails-to-Trails Conservancy; *page 51:* Rails-to-Trails Conservancy; *page 53:* Cam Fu; *page 57:* Mia Barbera; *page 59:* John Wells; *page 63:* Eckart Schmidt; *page 67:* Pat Strosahl; *page 69:* Eldan Goldenberg; *page 75:* Jan Tik; *page 79:* Mia Barbera; *page 83:* Eckart Schmidt; *page 87:* Barbara Richey/Rails-to-Trails Conservancy; *page 89:* Ted Murray; *page 93:* Barbara Richey/Rails-to-Trails Conservancy; *page 95:* Joe Mabel; *pages 99 and 103:* Barbara Richey/Rails-to-Trails Conservancy; *page 105:* Mia Barbera; *page 109:* Craig Hanchey; *page 11:* Barbara Richey/Rails-to-Trails Conservancy; *page 115:* Mia Barbera; *page 117:* Robert Ashworth; *page 119:* Rails-to-Trails Conservancy; *page 121:* Karl Wirsing; *page 123:* Larry Buchholz; *page 127:* Jeff Stevens; *page 129:* Teri Ruch/Friends of Trees; *page 133:* Cheryl Hill; *page 125:* Chuck Morlock; *page 139:* Stacey Malstrom; *page 143:* Bryce Hall; *page 147:* Katie Kennedy.

Support Rails-to-Trails Conservancy

The nation's leader in helping communities transform unused rail lines and connecting corridors into multiuse trails, Rails-to-Trails Conservancy (RTC) depends on the support of its members and donors to create access to healthy outdoor experiences.

Your donation will help support programs and services that have helped put more than 22,000 rail-trail miles on the ground. Every day, RTC provides vital assistance to communities to develop and maintain trails throughout the country. In addition, RTC advocates for trail-friendly policies, promotes the benefits of rail-trails, and defends rail-trail laws in the courts.

Join online at **railstotrails.org,** or mail your donation to Rails-to-Trails Conservancy, 2121 Ward Court NW, Fifth Floor, Washington, D.C. 20037.

Rails-to-Trails Conservancy is a 501(c)(3) nonprofit organization, and contributions are tax deductible.